First published in USA 1984
by Exeter Books
Distributed by Bookthrift
Exeter is a trademark of Simon & Schuster, Inc.
Bookthrift is a registered trademark of
Simon & Schuster, Inc. New York, New York

ISBN 0-671-07178-5

Printed in Italy Vallardi Industrie Grafiche, Milan

Picture Encyclopedia of
THE WORLD
for Children

Brian Williams and Lyn Williamson

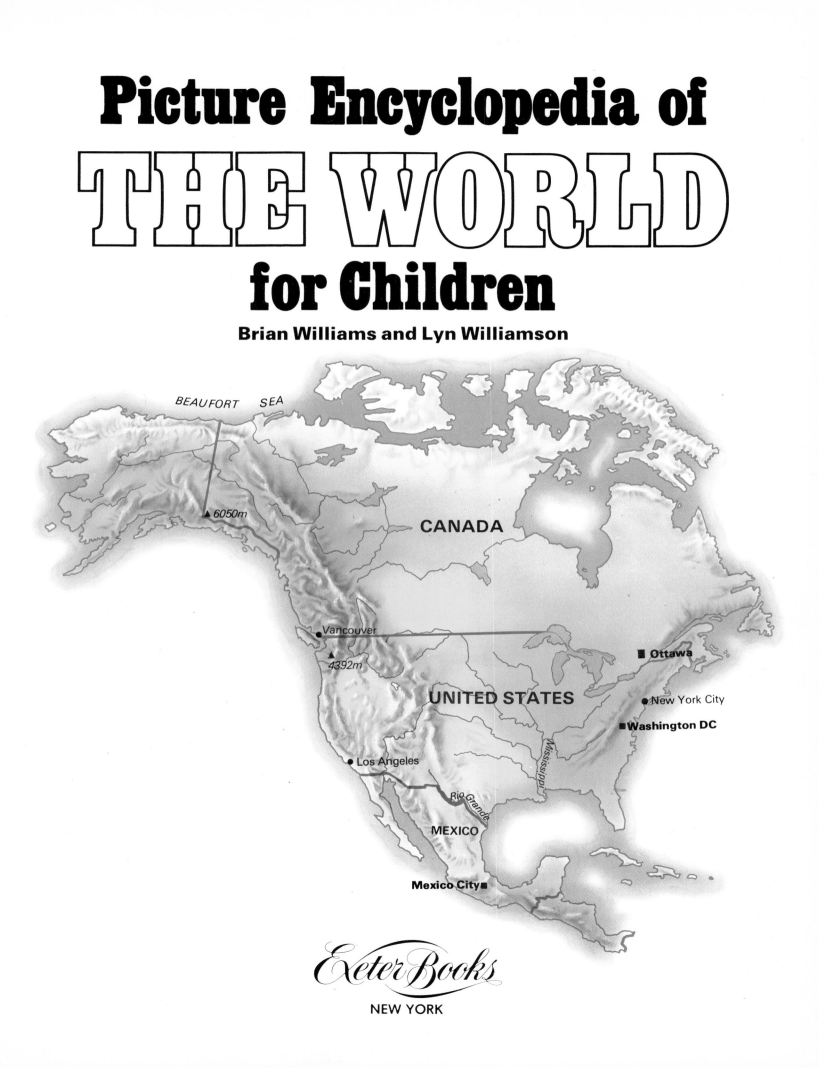

BEAUFORT SEA

▲ 6050m

CANADA

● Vancouver

▲ 4392m

UNITED STATES

■ Ottawa

● New York City

■ Washington DC

● Los Angeles

Mississippi

Rio Grande

MEXICO

Mexico City ■

Exeter Books

NEW YORK

Contents

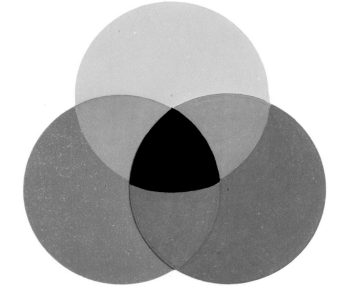

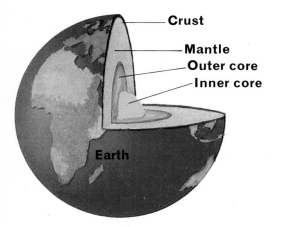

Crust
Mantle
Outer core
Inner core

Earth

Our Wonderful World

Our world is a whirling ball of rock. In the centre of the Earth is a solid *core* of metal. Around this inner core, it is so hot that the rock has melted in the outer core. The outer core is surrounded by hot, heavy rocks which form the *mantle*. The top layer of the Earth, called the *crust*, floats on the mantle. Here there are vast oceans and huge chunks of land called *continents*. There are seven continents. Each part of the world has its natural wonders and places where people have created great cities and shaped the land for their use.

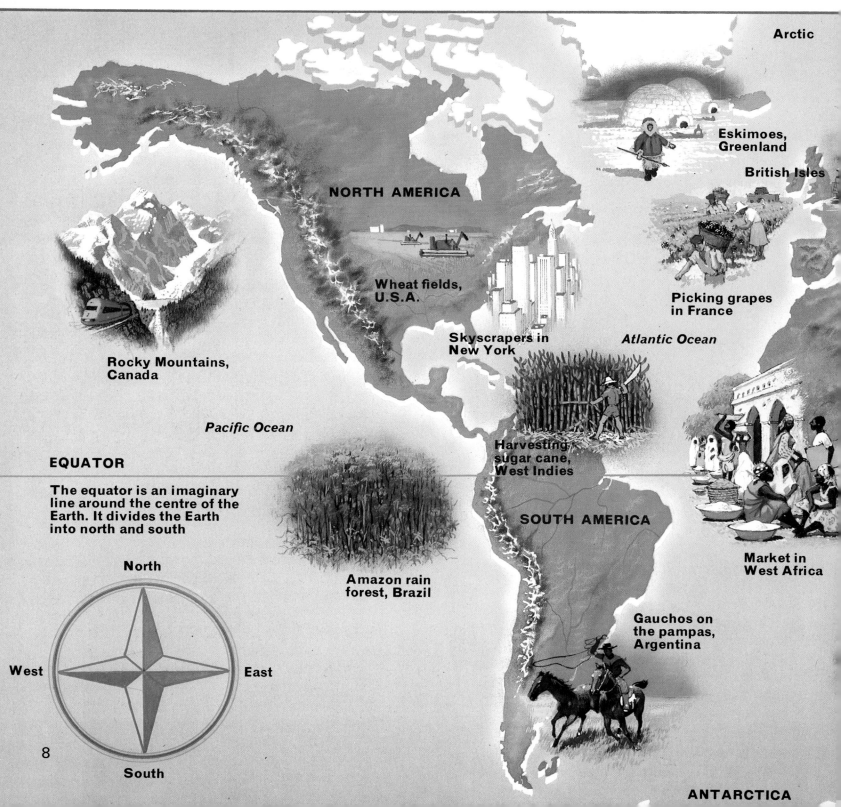

Arctic

Eskimoes, Greenland

British Isles

NORTH AMERICA

Wheat fields, U.S.A.

Picking grapes in France

Rocky Mountains, Canada

Skyscrapers in New York

Atlantic Ocean

Pacific Ocean

Harvesting sugar cane, West Indies

EQUATOR

The equator is an imaginary line around the centre of the Earth. It divides the Earth into north and south

SOUTH AMERICA

Market in West Africa

North

Amazon rain forest, Brazil

Gauchos on the pampas, Argentina

West

East

8

South

ANTARCTICA

The Earth is shaped rather like an orange with a flattened top and bottom. To look at the world we use a map. A map which shows all the Earth at the same time is made by taking the surface off the Earth, like peeling the skin off an orange and then opening it out flat.

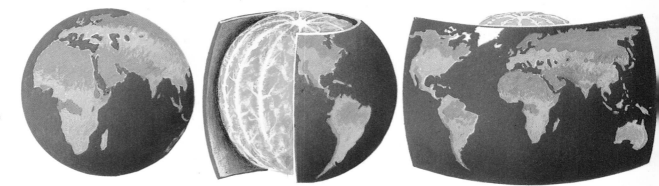

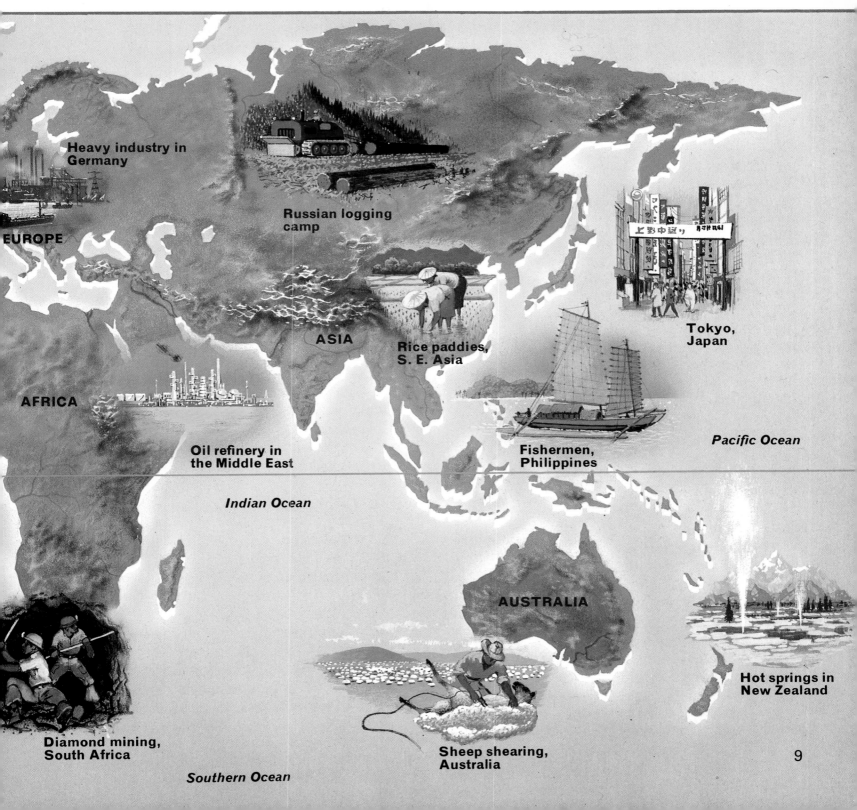

Heavy industry in Germany

Russian logging camp

EUROPE

Tokyo, Japan

ASIA

Rice paddies, S. E. Asia

AFRICA

Oil refinery in the Middle East

Fishermen, Philippines

Pacific Ocean

Indian Ocean

AUSTRALIA

Hot springs in New Zealand

Diamond mining, South Africa

Sheep shearing, Australia

Southern Ocean

9

Earth in Space

The Earth belongs to a family of planets spinning around the Sun. There are nine planets in the Sun's family. There are also mini-planets called *asteroids*.

Have you ever wondered why a ball comes down again when you throw it up into the air? It is because the Earth pulls everything down towards its centre. This pull is called *gravity*. Only a rocket with tremendous power can escape from the Earth's gravity and go off into space. The moon circles around the Earth because of the force of the Earth's gravity holding it like a magnet. The bigger a thing is the more gravity it has. The Sun is so big that it has a huge amount of gravity. It keeps the planets circling around it like a roundabout in space. It takes the Earth 365 days to make one journey around the Sun. This is our year. Other planets have longer or shorter years because they take longer or shorter times to go once around the Sun.

The Sun is a star. Without its warmth and light, there would be no life on Earth. There are millions and millions of other stars. Clusters of stars are called *galaxies*. We live in the Milky Way galaxy. Perhaps other beings live on far-away planets in other galaxies. No-one knows.

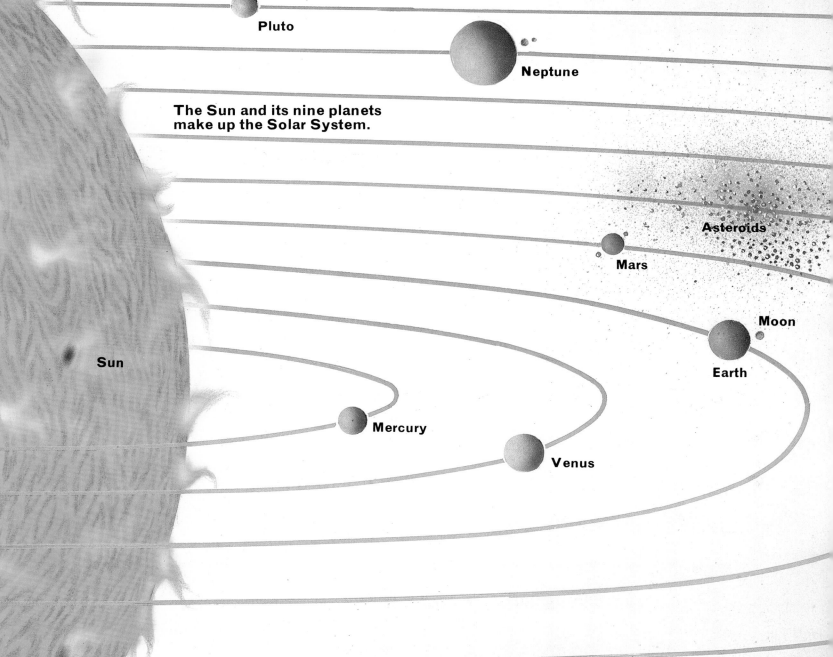

Pluto

Neptune

The Sun and its nine planets make up the Solar System.

Asteroids

Mars

Moon

Earth

Sun

Mercury

Venus

**Skylab
in space**

There is no air in space. So an
astronaut must carry oxygen to
breathe. Because there is very
little gravity in space, an
astronaut floats. A spacewalker
must stay tied to the spacecraft.
One push would send him
drifting off into space for ever.

Jupiter

Saturn

Uranus

The arrow shows the position of our Sun in the
Milky Way galaxy.

The Milky Way galaxy, shown by the arrow,
is only one of millions of galaxies.

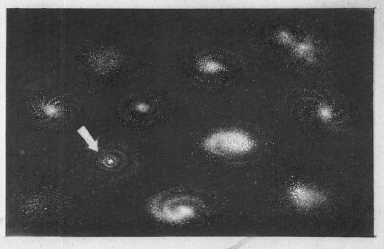

11

All Around the Year

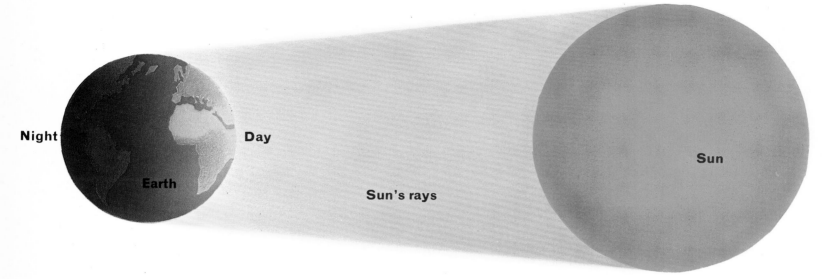

Night   **Day**   **Sun**

Earth   **Sun's rays**

Every 24 hours we have a day and a night. And every year the seasons change, from spring to summer, to autumn and winter. These changes are caused by the way the Earth moves.
The Earth travels around the Sun. At the same time it spins on its *axis*. Think of the axis as a rod pushed through the Earth from top to bottom, from the North Pole to the South Pole. The side of the Earth facing the Sun has day. The side turned away from the Sun has night. It takes 24 hours for the Earth to spin around once.

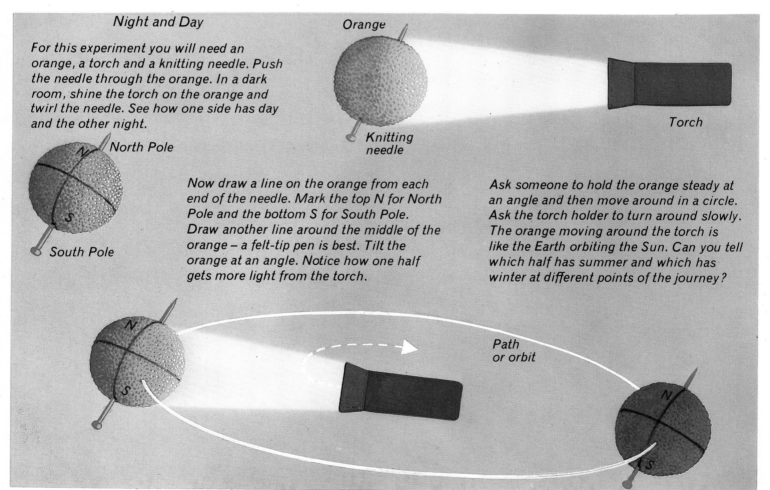

Night and Day

For this experiment you will need an orange, a torch and a knitting needle. Push the needle through the orange. In a dark room, shine the torch on the orange and twirl the needle. See how one side has day and the other night.

Orange

Knitting needle

Torch

North Pole

South Pole

Now draw a line on the orange from each end of the needle. Mark the top N for North Pole and the bottom S for South Pole. Draw another line around the middle of the orange – a felt-tip pen is best. Tilt the orange at an angle. Notice how one half gets more light from the torch.

Ask someone to hold the orange steady at an angle and then move around in a circle. Ask the torch holder to turn around slowly. The orange moving around the torch is like the Earth orbiting the Sun. Can you tell which half has summer and which has winter at different points of the journey?

Path or orbit

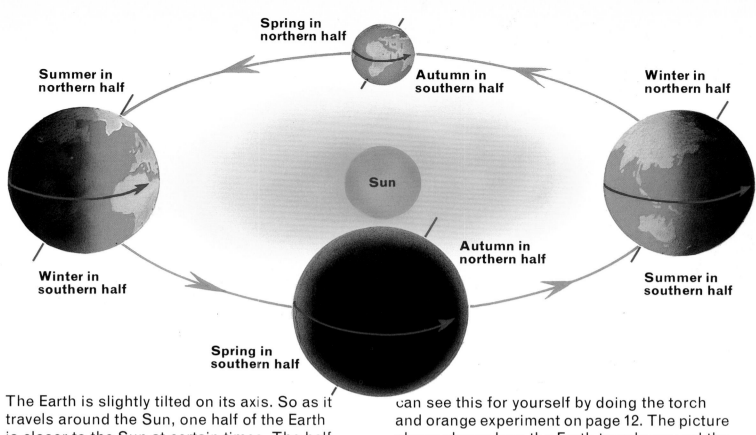

Spring in northern half

Autumn in southern half

Summer in northern half

Winter in northern half

Sun

Winter in southern half

Autumn in northern half

Summer in southern half

Spring in southern half

The Earth is slightly tilted on its axis. So as it travels around the Sun, one half of the Earth is closer to the Sun at certain times. The half that is closer gets more heat and so has summer. The half that is tilted away from the Sun gets less heat and so has winter. You can see this for yourself by doing the torch and orange experiment on page 12. The picture above shows how the Earth travels around the Sun. Twice during the year the halves of the Earth get equal heat from the Sun. Then one half has spring and the other half has autumn.

The seasons of the year change as the Earth travels around the Sun.

Winter

Spring

Summer

Autumn

13

Rain, Wind and Sun

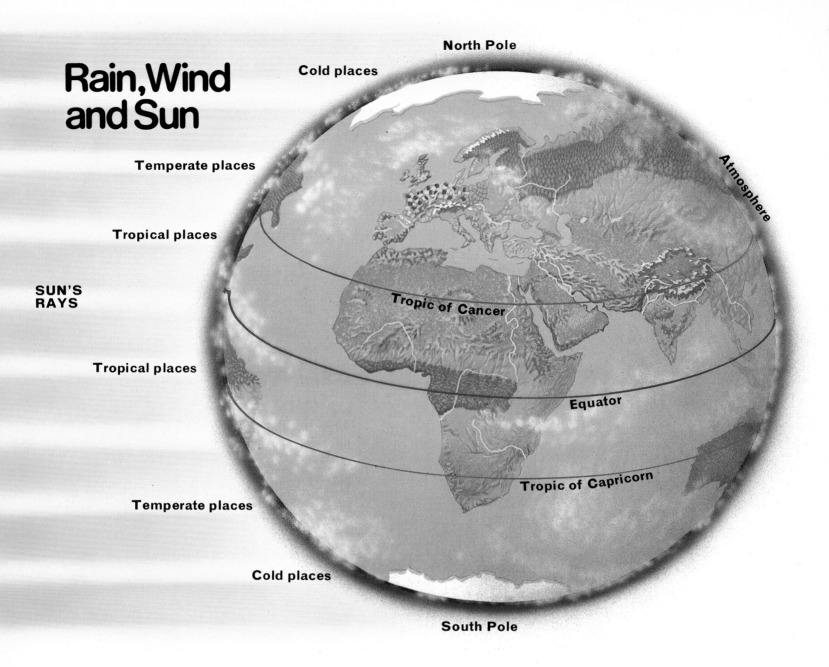

North Pole

Cold places

Temperate places

Atmosphere

Tropical places

SUN'S RAYS

Tropic of Cancer

Tropical places

Equator

Tropic of Capricorn

Temperate places

Cold places

South Pole

The Sun gives us heat and light. The picture above shows how the Sun's rays pass through the Earth's atmosphere to the surface of the Earth. The atmosphere is a layer of air around the Earth. It protects us from the fierce heat of the Sun and from dangerous rays that come from the Sun. Near the poles, the top and bottom of the world, the Sun's rays have to pass through more atmosphere and cover a larger area. These places are very cold and covered with ice all the year. As you go towards the middle of the Earth it gets warmer in the temperate regions. The hottest places are the tropics on either side of the equator.

Much of the Earth is covered by clouds, blown about by winds. Each cloud contains millions of tiny drops of water, sucked up as water vapour from the ground. The more water vapour a cloud picks up, the larger it becomes. Finally the drops of water become too heavy to float and they fall as rain.

Winds are moving currents of air. When air gets hot, it swells and becomes lighter. Then cooler, heavier air pushes into its place. This movement makes winds. Some winds blow steadily in great circles around the Earth. The most violent winds bring storms or gales. Warm winds from the sea often bring rain. A mixture of warm and cold air can cause fog. During a thunderstorm electrical sparks crackle in the dark clouds. Thunder is the noise made by the sparks. Lightning is the flash of the sparks themselves.

Why does it Rain?

The water vapour cools and makes clouds.

There is so much water in the clouds that it falls as rain

Some rain water flows back to the sea.

The Sun heats the water. Water goes into the air – evaporates – and then rises.

Because light travels much faster than sound, we always see the lightning before we hear the roll of thunder.

Snowflake

Frost

Dew

As the night air cools, dew forms. In very cold weather, water vapour can freeze and appear as frost or snow.

Weather

The weather affects animals and plants in many ways. People have always wanted to be able to forecast the weather. But for a long time they could only study the weather by looking up at the sky or, later, by using instruments like the ones below. However, today weather satellites keep watch from high up in the Earth's atmosphere. They report on any changes in the pattern of weather and tell us about high winds and storms.

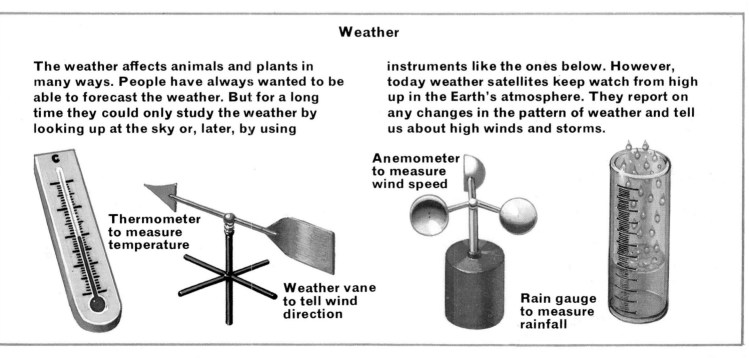

Thermometer to measure temperature

Weather vane to tell wind direction

Anemometer to measure wind speed

Rain gauge to measure rainfall

Water Everywhere

Tomato

Egg

The Earth from the Pacific side

Nearly three-quarters of the Earth's surface is covered by water. A spaceman looking down on the Pacific Ocean side would think that there was hardly any land at all.

Did you know that your body is also about three-quarters water? So are many of the foods we eat, such as eggs and tomatoes. We could not live without water. Most of the water which comes out of the taps at home began its journey as rain or snow. The water we use is collected from rivers and streams into lakes called *reservoirs*. The water is piped to waterworks where it is cleaned. Then underground pipes carry the water to homes and factories.

In the picture you can follow the story of a river, from its beginning where a glacier melts to its arrival at the sea.

Industrial town

Barges transport goods on rivers and canals

Harbour

Cargo ships

Waste from factories can poison or pollute a river

Yachts

A glacier is a huge river of ice

Waterfall

Reservoir built to supply water to factories and homes

A hydro-electric power station where the power of falling water is used to make electricity

Canyons

A canal is a man-made river

River

Lake

Irrigation ditches

Farmland

A delta often forms where a large river meets the sea

17

All Sorts of Places

In the desert no rain may fall for months, or even years. Where there is water, an oasis forms. Sometimes oil can be found under the ground.

The Polar lands are always cold. Snow and ice cover the ground. Winters are long and summers short.

North and south of the equator you can find tropical rain forests. These areas are hot and wet. Many people live in clearings.

Almost a fifth of the world's lands is covered by mountains. Mountain areas are often called *alpine*. People live in the sheltered valleys.

In the temperate lands of North America and Asia are wide grasslands. The land is flat and ideal for growing wheat.

Huge forests of evergreen conifer trees stretch across North America and northern Europe and Asia.

Maps and Map-making

Our Earth is one of nine planets circling around the Sun. It is the fifth largest planet in the Solar System. The Earth is shaped like a ball. But it is slightly flattened at the top and bottom.
We can show the Earth's land and seas as they are by drawing a map on the surface of a *globe*. A globe is a round ball, shaped like the Earth. You can see a picture of a globe on the right. When it turns, we can see all the sides one by one. Look at these four views of the same globe.

▲ A globe

Western

Eastern

Northern

Southern

But if we want to show all the Earth's sides at once on flat paper, we have to draw a *projection*. A projection is a flat drawing of rounded sections of the globe. It is impossible to lay a curved surface flat without twisting and pulling some of the sections. Try drawing a picture on an orange. Then peel the orange in segments and flatten them on a table. You will not be able to do it without squashing the peel out of shape, or *distorting* it. What has happened to your drawing? It is distorted. All maps of the world are distorted in one way or another.

The surface of the globe being peeled off.

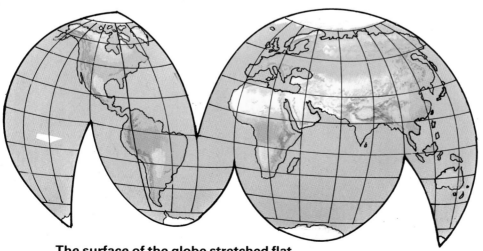

The surface of the globe stretched flat.

▲ Above and left you can see one method of peeling the surface off a globe to make a flat map. The lines on the map running from north to south are lines of *longitude.* The lines running from east to west are the lines of *latitude*. These lines are very useful. Map-makers use them to make sure that cities and boundaries are put in the right place on the map.

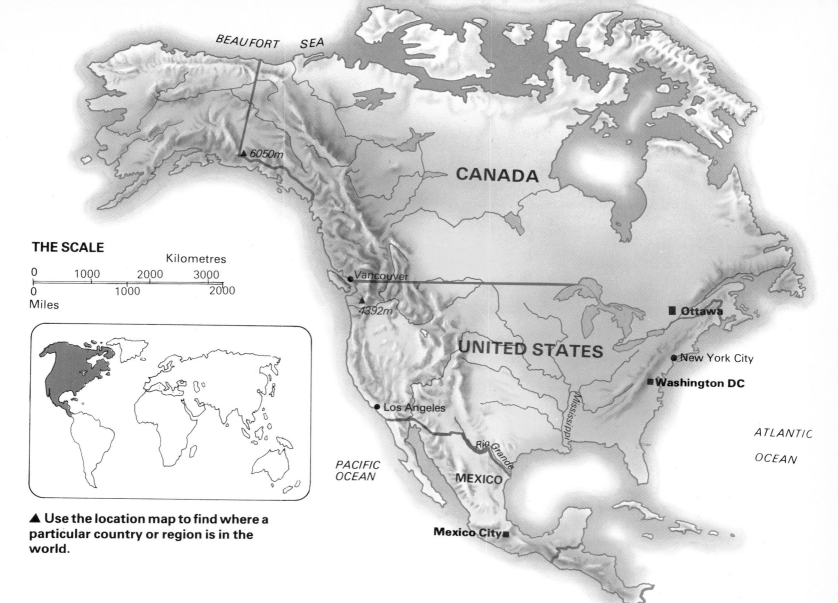

BEAUFORT SEA

▲ 6050m

CANADA

THE SCALE

Kilometres

0   1000   2000   3000

0   1000   2000

Miles

● Vancouver

▲ 4392m

UNITED STATES

■ Ottawa

● New York City

■ Washington DC

● Los Angeles

Mississippi

ATLANTIC

OCEAN

Rio Grande

PACIFIC
OCEAN

MEXICO

Mexico City ■

▲ Use the location map to find where a
particular country or region is in the
world.

How To Use a Map

Many kinds of maps can be drawn. They give us
different information. A *political* map, like the
one inside the back cover of this book, shows
the boundaries of the world's countries. The
physical map inside the front cover shows the
land's surface with its oceans, rivers, lakes and
mountains. Colours and *symbols* are used on
maps to give information. Look at the map
above. To see what the colours and symbols
mean, check the *key* on the right.

Maps are much smaller than the actual area of
the countries they show. But they are always
drawn to *scale*. Scale means the comparison
between the map size and the real size. If the
scale is written like this – 1:800,000, it means that
one centimetre on the map stands for 800,000
centimetres (8 kilometres) on the ground. The
maps in this atlas have a bar scale. You can
measure any distance on the map, then compare
it to the bar scale to find the real land distance.

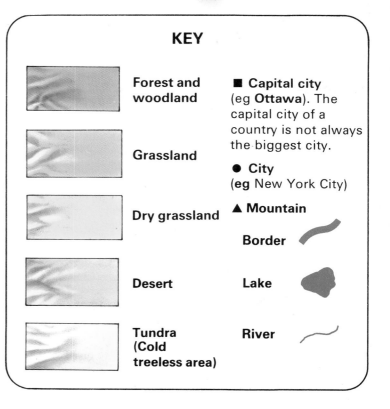

KEY

Forest and
woodland

Grassland

Dry grassland

Desert

Tundra
(Cold
treeless area)

■ **Capital city**
(eg **Ottawa**). The
capital city of a
country is not always
the biggest city.

● **City**
(eg New York City)

▲ **Mountain**

Border

Lake

River

Countries of the World

Greenland

ICELAND

Alaska

C A N A D A

UNITED KINGDOM

IRELAND

UNITED STATES OF AMERICA

FRANCE

SPAIN

PORTUGAL

25

MOROCCO

ALGER

TROPIC OF CANCER

MEXICO

BAHAMAS

CUBA

56

MAURITANIA

MALI

CAPE VERDE ISLANDS

26

46

53

DOMINICA
ST LUCIA
BARBADOS

48

54 55

27

29

32

50

57

28

BENIN

47

52

30

GHANA

49

VENEZUELA

58

31

IVORY COAST

51

59 60

COLOMBIA

33

EQUATOR

ECUADOR

35

PERU

BRAZIL

BOLIVIA

PARAGUAY

TROPIC OF CAPRICORN

URUGUAY

ARGENTINA

C H I L E

Falkland Islands

1 DENMARK	11 YUGOSLAVIA
2 NETHERLANDS	12 ALBANIA
3 BELGIUM	13 CYPRUS
4 LUXEMBOURG	14 LEBANON
5 W. GERMANY	15 ISRAEL
6 E. GERMANY	16 SYRIA
7 SWITZERLAND	17 JORDAN
8 AUSTRIA	18 KUWAIT
9 CZECHOSLOVAKIA	19 BAHRAIN
10 HUNGARY	20 UNITED ARAB EMIRATES

NORWAY
SWEDEN
FINLAND
POLAND
9
8 10
11
12
GREECE
ITALY
BULGARIA
ROMANIA
TURKEY
13→ 16
15
14→
17
LIBYA
EGYPT
18
SAUDI
ARABIA
19
QATAR
20
OMAN
NIGER
CHAD
SUDAN
21 YEMEN P.D.R.
41
SOMALI
REPUBLIC
ETHIOPIA
34
39 38
KENYA
CONGO
ZAIRE
40
TANZANIA
ANGOLA
42
ZAMBIA
MOZAMBIQUE
MADAGASCAR
43
NAMIBIA
BOTSWANA
SOUTH
AFRICA
44
45

U   S   S   R

MONGOLIA
CHINA
NORTH
KOREA
SOUTH
KOREA
JAPAN
IRAN
AFGHAN-
ISTAN
IRAQ
PAKISTAN
NEPAL
22
BURMA
23
TAIWAN
INDIA
LAOS
HONG
KONG
VIETNAM
THAILAND
24
PHILIPPINES
SRI LANKA
MALDIVE
ISLANDS
BRUNEI
MALAYSIA
SINGAPORE
INDONESIA
PAPUA
NEW
GUINEA
SOLOMON
ISLANDS
SEYCHELLES
VANUATU
FIJI
NEW
CALEDONIA
AUSTRALIA
NEW
ZEALAND

21 YEMEN A.R.	31 LIBERIA	41 DJIBOUTI	51 COSTA RICA
22 BHUTAN	32 UPPER VOLTA	42 MALAWI	52 PANAMA
23 BANGLADESH	33 TOGO	43 ZIMBABWE	53 JAMAICA
24 KAMPUCHEA	34 CENTRAL AFRICAN REPUBLIC	44 SWAZILAND	54 HAITI
25 TUNISIA	35 EQUATORIAL GUINEA	45 LESOTHO	55 DOMINICAN REPUBLIC
26 SENEGAL	36 GABON	46 BELIZE	56 PUERTO RICO
27 GAMBIA	37 CAMEROON	47 GUATEMALA	57 TRINIDAD AND TOBAGO
28 GUINEA-BISSAU	38 UGANDA	48 HONDURAS	58 GUYANA
29 GUINEA	39 RWANDA	49 EL SALVADOR	59 SURINAM
30 SIERRA LEONE	40 BURUNDI	50 NICARAGUA	60 FRENCH GUIANA

Scandinavia

During the Ice Ages, Scandinavia was covered with ice sheets and glaciers. These cut deep *fiords* into the coastline and formed many lakes and islands. Iceland is the most northern country in Europe. It still has many snowfields. It is also dotted with many hot springs, steaming geysers and over 100 volcanoes.

Most Scandinavians enjoy a high standard of living. Sweden is the largest and richest of the countries. Over half the Swedish people live in modern cities, such as Stockholm and Goteborg. Many earn their living by manufacturing paper and other wood products. Sweden, Norway and Finland have large areas of forest.

Scandinavia's coastal waters teem with fish. Fishermen, mainly from Iceland and Norway, catch large quantities of cod and herring which are canned or frozen in fish-processing factories. Dairy farming is important in Denmark. Only one-fifth of the people are farmers, but they use the latest machinery and farming methods.

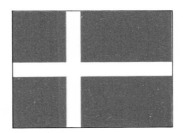

▲ The flag of Denmark
▶ The flag of Finland
▼ The flag of Norway

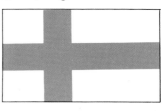

▲ The flag of Sweden

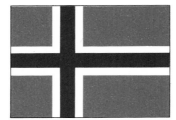

▼ Buttermaking in a Danish factory. Denmark is a major world producer of butter.

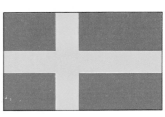

▲ Special trains are used in Finland throughout the long winter to sweep the tracks clear of snow.

▼ The coast of Norway is broken by hundreds of fiords. Inland you can see a hydro-electric power station. It uses the force of water, falling down the cliffs, to make electricity. On the right of the picture are the lakes and forests of the Swedish countryside. Sweden borders Norway.

▲ Swimmers in Iceland can bathe in the open air in the middle of winter. Hot springs heat the pool.

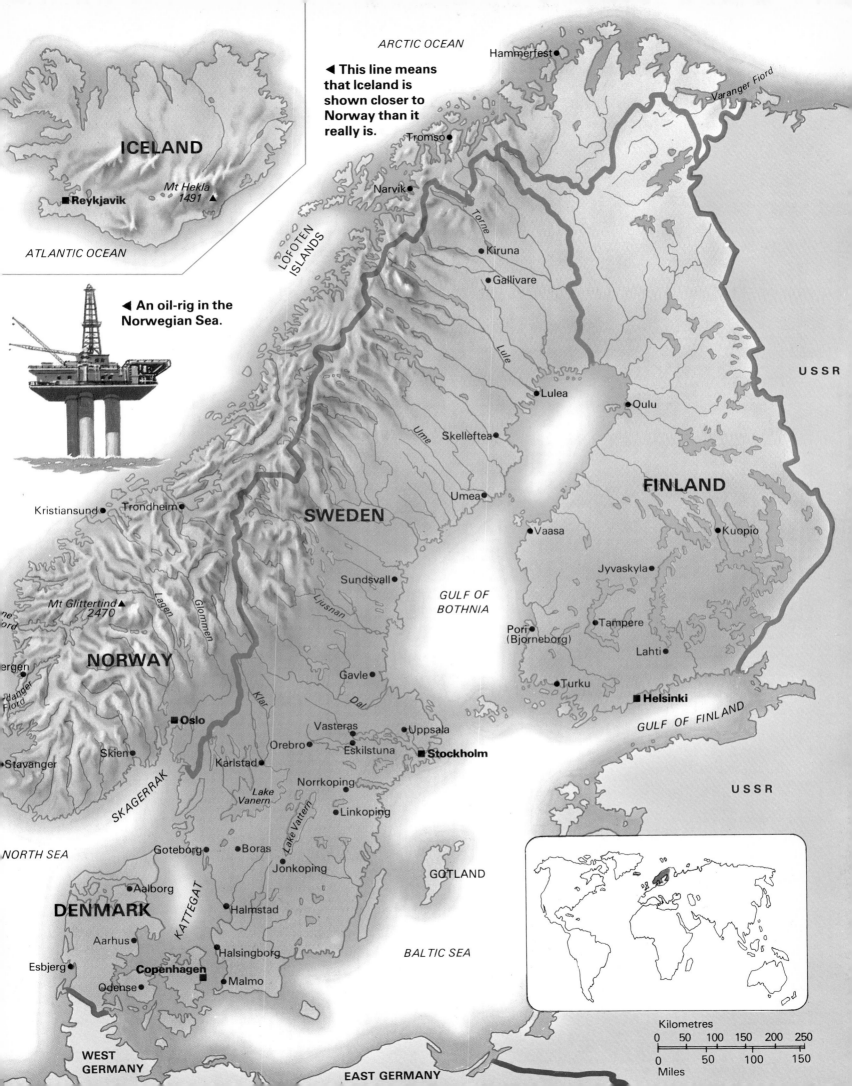

ARCTIC OCEAN

Hammerfest

◄ **This line means that Iceland is shown closer to Norway than it really is.**

Varanger Fiord

ICELAND

Mt Hekla
1491 ▲

■ **Reykjavik**

ATLANTIC OCEAN

Tromso

Narvik

LOFOTEN
ISLANDS

Torne

Kiruna

Gallivare

◄ **An oil-rig in the Norwegian Sea.**

Lule

Lulea

Oulu

U S S R

Ume

Skelleftea

Kristiansund

Trondheim

Umea

FINLAND

SWEDEN

Vaasa

Kuopio

Mt Glittertind ▲
2470

Lagen

Glommen

Sundsvall

**GULF OF
BOTHNIA**

Jyvaskyla

NORWAY

Ljusnan

Pori
(Bjorneborg)

Tampere

ergen

Lahti

der
Fiord

Klar

Gavle

Dal

Turku

■ **Oslo**

■ **Helsinki**

Skien

Vasteras

Uppsala

GULF OF FINLAND

Stavanger

Orebro

Eskilstuna

■ **Stockholm**

Karlstad

Norrkoping

*Lake
Vanern*

Lake Vattern

Linkoping

U S S R

SKAGERRAK

NORTH SEA

Goteborg

Boras

GOTLAND

Jonkoping

Aalborg

KATTEGAT

Halmstad

DENMARK

BALTIC SEA

Aarhus

Halsingborg

Esbjerg

Copenhagen ■

Odense

Malmo

**WEST
GERMANY**

EAST GERMANY

Kilometres
0 50 100 150 200 250

0 50 100 150
Miles

The Netherlands, Belgium and Luxembourg

The Netherlands, Belgium and Luxembourg are known as the Low Countries because much of the land is flat and below sea-level. In the Netherlands high *dykes*, or sea walls, have been built around low-lying lands, which are called *polders.* Nearly a quarter of the Netherlands's land has been *reclaimed*, or taken back, from the sea in this way.

The Low Countries have a combined population of 23 million. This makes them the most densely populated group of countries in Europe. They are also wealthy countries. Most people work in offices and factories, often in textile and electrical companies. Others work on the land. The farms are small and very modern. Dutch farmers grow either flowers or vegetables or keep cows. There are also large iron and steel mills in Belgium and Luxembourg.

Luxembourgers are *bi-lingual.* They speak two languages — French and Luxemburgish.

▲ The flags of the Netherlands, above, and of Luxembourg, below. The Netherlands is often known as Holland.

▲ Windmills were once used in Holland to pump water from the polders.

▼ There are many fine, old buildings in Brussels, such as these in the Grand Place. The headquarters of the Common Market (the EEC) are also in Brussels.

▲ The Port of Rotterdam is situated on the Rhine. It is one of the busiest ports in the world.

▼ The Dutch countryside is divided into small farms. Canals form an inland waterway system.

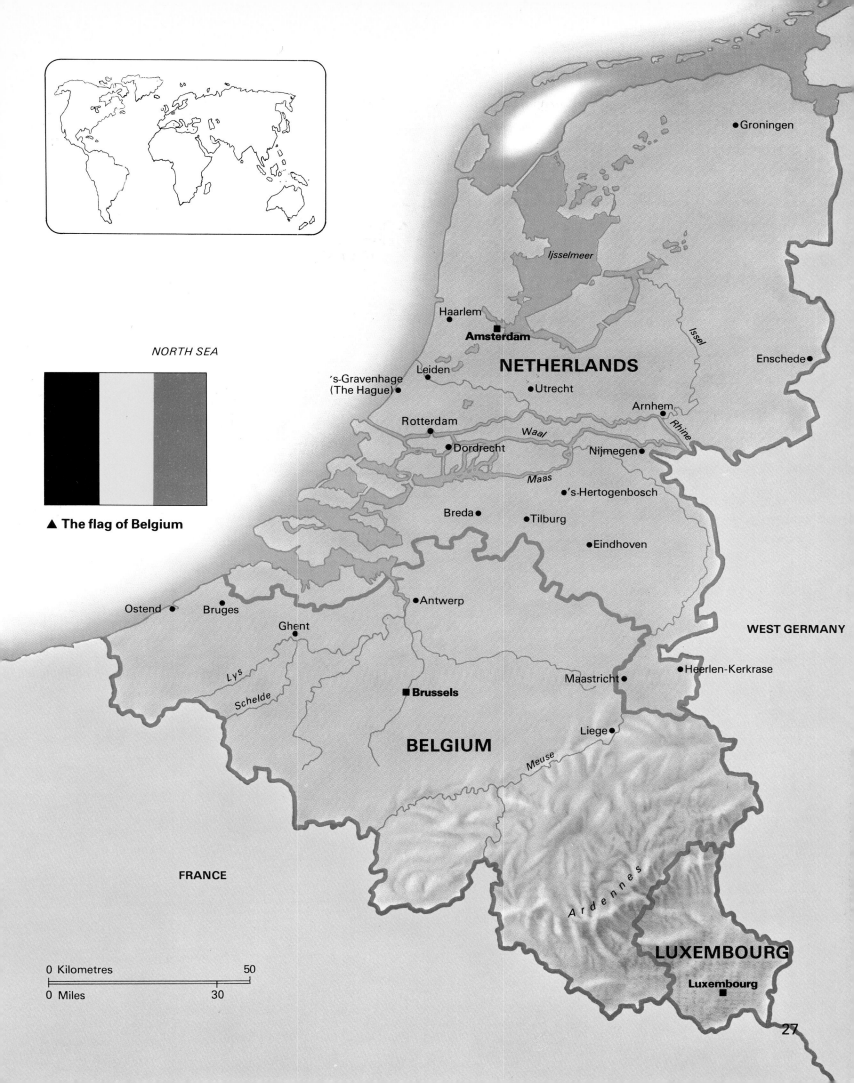

NORTH SEA

▲ The flag of Belgium

Groningen

Ijsselmeer

Haarlem

Amsterdam

NETHERLANDS

Leiden

Enschede

's-Gravenhage
(The Hague)

Utrecht

Issel

Arnhem

Rotterdam

Rhine

Waal

Dordrecht

Nijmegen

Maas

's-Hertogenbosch

Breda

Tilburg

Eindhoven

Antwerp

Ostend

Bruges

WEST GERMANY

Ghent

Heerlen-Kerkrase

Lys

Schelde

Brussels

Maastricht

Liege

BELGIUM

Meuse

FRANCE

A
r
d
e
n
n
e
s

LUXEMBOURG

0 Kilometres   50

0 Miles   30

Luxembourg

27

Great Britain and the Republic of Ireland

The United Kingdom of Great Britain and Ireland consists of England, Scotland, Wales and Northern Ireland. Many people call the United Kingdom simply Britain. The Republic of Ireland or Eire was once part of the United Kingdom. But in 1921 it became a separate country.

A moist climate makes Britain and the Republic of Ireland ideal for farming. But in Britain one-third of the food must still be *imported*. This means it must be bought from other countries. The farms are too small to feed the large population.

Industry is very important in Britain. For every one person working on the land, there are ten people living and working in cities. Britain pays for the food it imports by selling manufactured products, such as cars and machinery, to other countries.

Britain is divided into many different districts with their own customs and *dialects*, or ways of speaking. In Wales children learn Welsh as well as English in schools.

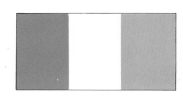

▲ The flag of the United Kingdom. Over 56 million people live in the UK. The capital is London in the south of England.

▲ The flag of the Republic of Ireland. Over three million people live in this country and their capital is Dublin.

▲ A coal mine in Wales. Coal was once a main source of fuel. But it is now being replaced by oil, gas and nuclear power.

▼ Many Irish farmers rear cattle, sheep and pigs on small farms, like this one. But farms are becoming more modern.

▲ The Beefeaters used to guard the Tower of London where kings and queens have been imprisoned in the past.

▶ Find Britain and the Irish Republic on this world location map.

◀ This peaceful, fairytale cottage is in the English countryside. But most people in Britain live in towns and cities.

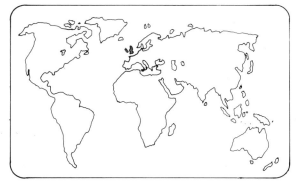

ORKNEY
ISLANDS

SHETLAND ISLANDS

John o'
Groats

▲ A Scottish trawler.

▲ An oil-rig explores the
British oil-field in the North
Sea.

H E B R I D E S

Inverness
Loch Ness
Dee
Aberdeen

North West Highlands

▲ Ben Nevis
1347m

G r a m p i a n s

Tay

Dundee

SCOTLAND

Loch
Lomond

Glasgow   Edinburgh

Clyde

N O R T H

S E A

Londonderry

NORTHERN
IRELAND

Belfast

Tyne

Newcastle

Pennines

Eden

Lake
District

ISLE OF MAN

Lough
Mask

Central   Plains

Dublin ■

I R I S H

S E A

York
Leeds   Hull

Liverpool   Manchester

Sheffield

Shannon

Lough
Derg

Wicklow
Mts

Snowdon
1086m

Nottingham   Trent

REPUBLIC OF
IRELAND (EIRE)

Barrow

Cambrian Mts

Birmingham

Severn

The
Fens

Ouse   Great
Yarmouth

Cambridge

Mts of
Kerry

Cork

WALES

ENGLAND

Cotswolds

Avon

Oxford   Chiltern Hills

A T L A N T I C

Swansea

Cardiff

Thames   London ■

Bristol

North   Downs   Canterbury

O C E A N

Bath

Dover

Exmoor

Southampton   Portsmouth

Brighton

Bournemouth

Isle of Wight

Dartmoor

Plymouth

E N G L I S H   C H A N N E L

Kilometres
0 20 40 60 80 100

0   25   50
Miles

ISLES OF
SCILLY

Land's
End

FRANCE

CHANNEL ISLANDS

France

France is the second largest country in Europe. Along most of its borders there are mountain ranges. The Jura Mountains separate France from Switzerland, the Pyrenees separate it from Spain, and the Vosges separate France partly from Germany. Find the Alps on the map. They border France with Italy and contain Mont Blanc, which is the highest peak in France.

Although many French people work in factories, farming is very important. The warm climate and rich soil help farmers to grow cereals, fruit and sugar-beet. Grapes, used for making wine, are grown in most regions. But the main grapevine growing areas are in Bordeaux, Burgundy and Champagne. Dairy farming is also important and over 300 different cheeses are made.

Paris, Lyon and Marseille are the main cities in France. Painters and writers from all over the world have lived in Paris. Many tourists go there today to see its historic buildings, which include the Louvre and the Notre Dame Cathedral.

▲ French cafes are not just places for eating and drinking. They are like a club. People meet their friends there and linger talking or reading. In summer chairs and tables are put outside.

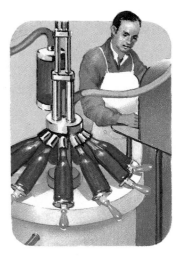

▲ These modern machines fill bottles with wine on a vineyard. Experts taste and approve the wine before it is bottled. Most wine tastes better if it is left to mature for several years.

◄ Workers in this factory near Paris assemble cars on a conveyor belt. Large numbers of cars and aeroplanes are made in France each year.

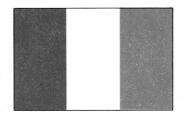

▲ The French flag. France is a republic, divided into many provinces. More than 54 million people live in France.

▼ Carcassonne Castle was built in medieval times. Its thick walls were designed to keep out invaders.

▼ The Eiffel Tower looms over Paris. It was built in 1889 for the Great Exhibition.

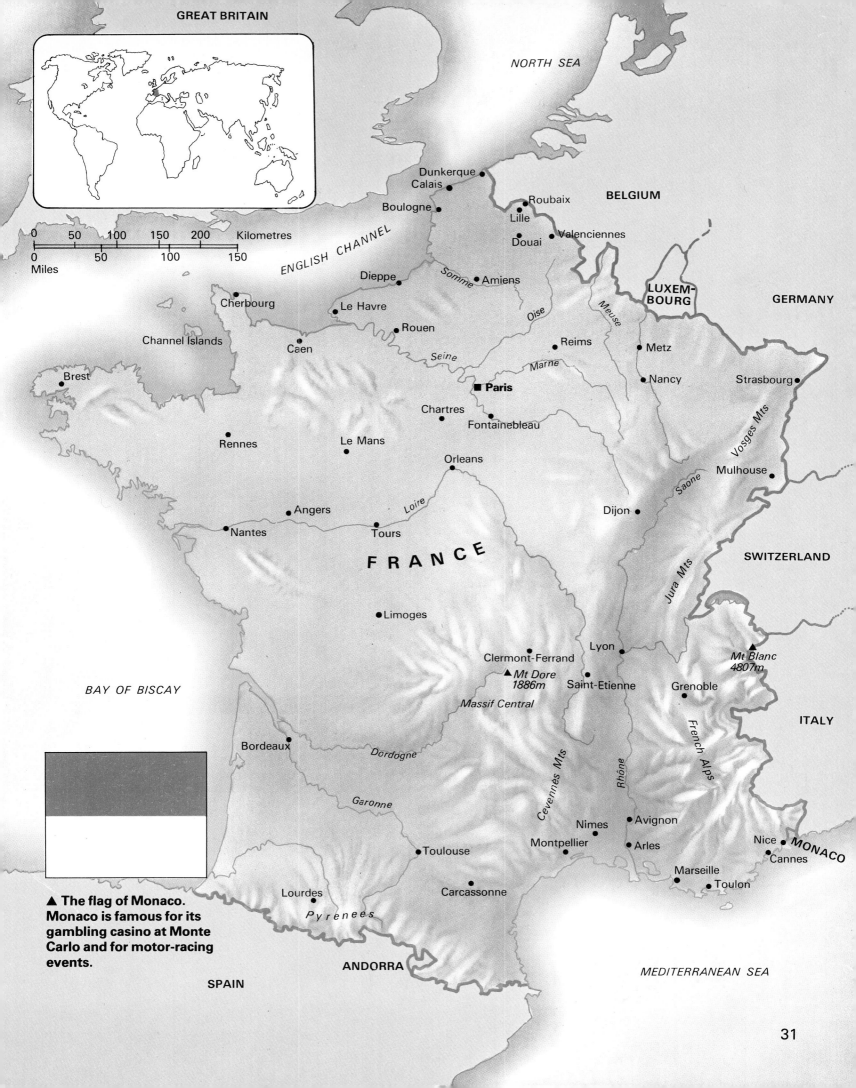

GREAT BRITAIN

NORTH SEA

0 50 100 150 200 Kilometres

0 50 100 150
Miles

ENGLISH CHANNEL

Dunkerque
Calais
Boulogne
Roubaix
Lille
Douai
Valenciennes

BELGIUM

LUXEM-
BOURG

GERMANY

Dieppe
Somme
Amiens
Oise
Meuse

Cherbourg
Le Havre
Rouen
Reims
Metz
Nancy
Strasbourg

Channel Islands
Caen
Seine
Marne
Vosges Mts

Brest
Paris
Chartres
Fontainebleau

Rennes
Le Mans
Orleans
Dijon
Saone
Mulhouse

Angers
Loire
Tours

Nantes

FRANCE

Jura Mts

SWITZERLAND

BAY OF BISCAY

Limoges

Lyon
Mt Blanc
4807m

Clermont-Ferrand
▲ Mt Dore
1886m
Saint-Etienne
Grenoble

Massif Central

French Alps

ITALY

Bordeaux
Dordogne

Cevennes Mts

Rhône

Garonne

Nimes
Avignon

Toulouse
Montpellier
Arles
Nice
MONACO
Cannes

Lourdes
Carcassonne
Marseille
Toulon

Pyrenees

▲ The flag of Monaco.
Monaco is famous for its
gambling casino at Monte
Carlo and for motor-racing
events.

SPAIN

ANDORRA

MEDITERRANEAN SEA

31

Germany-East and West

Since 1945, Germany has been divided into East Germany and West Germany. West Germany's proper name is the Federal Republic of Germany. East Germany's proper name is the German Democratic Republic. The city of Berlin is also divided into east and west *zones*. In 1961, a wall was built along East Berlin's boundaries to stop people crossing into West Germany.

The Germans are well-organized and hard-working people. Since 1945, large numbers of factories have been set up in both East and West Germany. These manufacture everything from steel to textiles. In West Germany, workers in the industrial Ruhr valley make cars, heavy machinery, cables and electrical equipment. Today West Germany is one of the wealthiest countries in Europe.

Farming as well as manufacturing is important in East Germany. There are also many *lignite* mines. Lignite is a type of coal. East Germany is the world's chief supplier of lignite. Workers mine around 250 million tonnes of it every year.

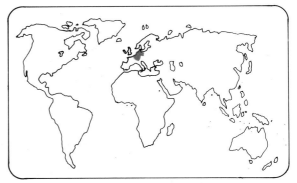

▲ The flags of West Germany, above, and of East Germany, right. Over 16 million people live in East Germany. Their capital is the east zone of Berlin. Nearly 62 million people live in West Germany and their capital is Bonn.

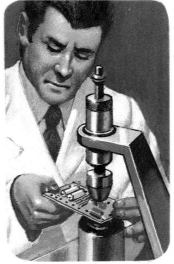

▶ This technician is working in an electronics factory in Dresden, East Germany.

▼ Barges travel down the Rhine in West Germany, past lovely towns and castles, green fields and vineyards. They pick up goods from industrial cities and carry them to other places in Europe.

Kilometres
0   50   100   150
0   30   60   90
Miles

BALTIC SEA

NORTH SEA

• Kiel

Kiel Canal

• Rostock

• Lubeck

• Hamburg

Elbe

POLAND

NETHERLANDS

Ems

• Bremen

Aller

Weser

• Hanover

• Brunswick

• Magdeburg

■ **Berlin**

Oder

Oder

EAST GERMANY

Spree

• Munster

• Bielefeld

Harz Mts

Rhine

Dortmund

Duisburg   Essen   • Bochum

Krefeld

Ruhr

• Wuppertal

Elbe

• Halle

1onchen-gladbach   Dusseldorf

• Kassel

• Leipzig

• Cologne

• Dresden

• Aachen

Karl-Marx-Stadt •

■ **Bonn**

WEST GERMANY

BELGIUM

LUXEMBOURG

Mosel

• Frankfurt

Wiesbaden •

• Mainz

Main

CZECHOSLOVAKIA

• Mannheim

• Nuremberg

• Saarbrucken

Rhine

• Karlsruhe

B l a c k   F o r e s t

• Stuttgart

Danube

FRANCE

• Augsburg

• Munich

33

AUSTRIA

SWITZERLAND

Spain and Portugal

Spain's interior is a vast *plateau*, which means an area of high flat ground. It is crossed by several mountain ranges. But the highest peaks are in the Pyrenees in the north and the Sierra Nevada in the south. Fertile plains and sandy beaches surround the central plateau. Spain is divided into several regions. One of these is Andalusia in the south. It is famous for its lively fiestas and gypsy flamenco dancers.

Spain's warm climate and golden sands attract thousands of tourists to its coastal resorts. Many Spaniards work in the tourist industry, but most work on the land. Some farmers do everything by hand or with the help of a donkey or mule. The soil is very dry and needs to be constantly watered, or *irrigated*. Farmers grow wheat, rice, olives, grapes and oranges.

Portugal borders Spain on the west. Most people are fishermen and farmers. Others work in the tourist industry or in factories where they process food and make textiles. There are large cork forests in Portugal and many vineyards. Cork and port, a special type of wine, are exported to countries all over the world.

▲ **A Portuguese fisherman mends his nets. Huge numbers of sardines are caught off Portugal's coast.**

▼ **Oranges are grown in Spain on plantations, called 'huertas'. Most of them are grown around Valencia.**

▲ **The flag of Spain. Find Andorra and Gibraltar on the map opposite. These two states and Spain and Portugal make up the Iberian Peninsula. The capital of Spain is Madrid. Most of the people are Roman Catholic.**

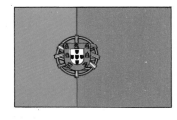

▲ **The flag of Portugal. Lisbon is the capital of Portugal.**

▶ **Benidorm on the Spanish Mediterranean coast is a holiday boom-town. Thousands of tourists from colder parts of Europe visit its sandy beaches and luxury hotels.**

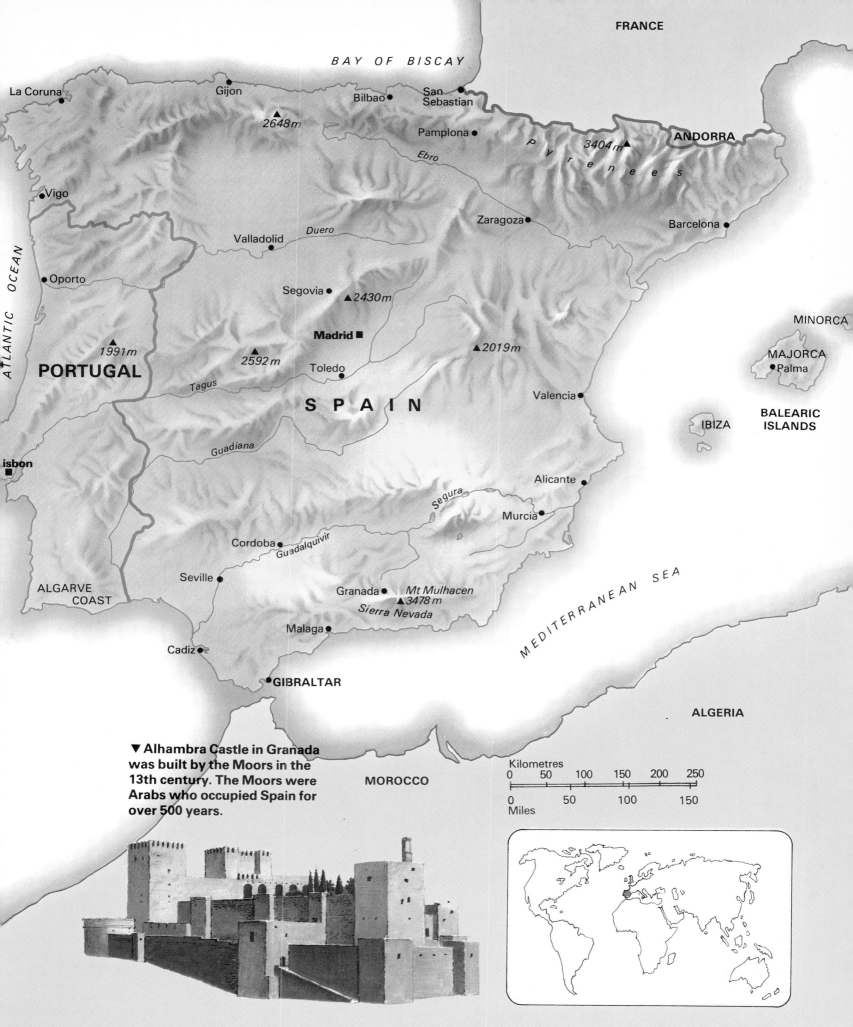

FRANCE

BAY OF BISCAY

La Coruna •   • Gijon   • Bilbao   • San
                  ▲   Sebastian

           2648m   • Pamplona   **ANDORRA**

                 Ebro   *3404m* ▲

• Vigo

         Duero   • Zaragoza   • Barcelona

• Oporto   • Valladolid

ATLANTIC OCEAN

          • Segovia   ▲*2430m*

    ▲   **Madrid** ■

    1991m   ▲*2019m*   MINORCA

PORTUGAL   ▲   • Toledo   MAJORCA

           2592 m   • Palma

          Tagus   **S P A I N**

                                       • Valencia   **BALEARIC**

         Guadiana   IBIZA   **ISLANDS**

■isbon

                             • Alicante

                 Segura

                       • Murcia

    • Cordoba   *Guadalquivir*

                                      MEDITERRANEAN SEA

• Seville

ALGARVE
COAST   Granada •   *Mt Mulhacen*
                           ▲ *3478 m*
                  Sierra Nevada

    • Malaga

• Cadiz

GIBRALTAR

                                         ALGERIA

▼ **Alhambra Castle in Granada**
was built by the Moors in the
13th century. The Moors were   **MOROCCO**
Arabs who occupied Spain for
over 500 years.

Kilometres
0   50   100   150   200   250

0   50   100   150
Miles

Italy and Switzerland

Look at Italy on the map and it will remind you of a boot kicking a ball. Sicily is the 'ball'. Notice too the Apennine Mountains running down the back of Italy like a spine. There are several volcanic mountains in Italy. The best known is Mount Vesuvius, near the city of Naples.

Tourists flock to Italy to enjoy the warm climate, to see the beautiful buildings and paintings, and to visit the ruins of Ancient Rome. In the north there are large industrial cities, such as Milan and Turin. Italians make textiles and cars for *export*, to sell to other countries. In the south farmers grow olives, citrus fruit, and grapes for making wine.

Switzerland is famous for its snow-capped Alps and shimmering lakes. It is called the 'playground of Europe' because each winter holiday-makers go there to ski. Nearly half the Swiss people work in factories making chemicals, scientific instruments, clocks and watches and delicious chocolate.

▲ **The Pope, the head of the Roman Catholic Church, speaks to a crowd in Vatican City.**

▼ **This man is checking a massive web, or roll of paper, in an Italian printing works.**

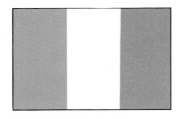

▲ **The flag of Italy**

◄ **A highly-skilled Swiss watchmaker peers through an eyeglass at the tiny pieces of a clock.**

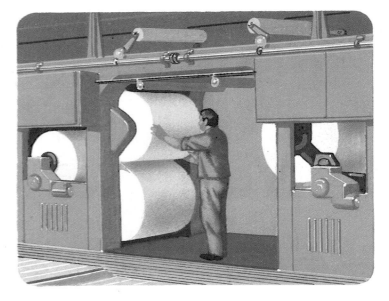

▼ **A volcanic mountain towers over the coast and rolling countryside of central Italy. There are farms and vineyards on either side of the mountain range. Olive groves stretch over the hilly areas.**

WEST GERMANY

AUSTRIA

SWITZERLAND

Basel

● Zurich

Jura Mts   Aare

● Luzern

■ **Berne**

Rhine

A   l   p   s

Lake Constance

▲4274 m

Lausanne

Rhone

▲ 4094 m

*Lake Leman
(L. Geneva)*

Matterhorn
▲4478 m

Lake Como

eneva●

4807 m▲

▲ 4634 m

▲4061 m

FRANCE

Milan ●

● Brescia

Lake Garda

Trieste

Verona ●

● Padua

● Venice

Turin ●

Po

YUGOSLAVIA

▲3841 m

Parma ●

● Ferrara

Modena ●

▲3297 m

● Genoa

● Bologna

2165 m▲   **ITALY**

● Rimini

ADRIATIC SEA

LIGURIAN SEA

● Pisa

● Florence

**SAN
MARINO**

Livorno ●

Siena ●

A
p
e
n

● Assisi

▲ 2478 m

Tiber

n

▲ 2710 m

**CORSICA
(France)**

n

▲ 2914 m

i

■ **Rome**

n

● Sassari

e

s

● Bari

**SARDINA
(Italy)**

1277 m

Naples ●

▲*Mt Vesuvius*

▲
1834 m

Capri ●

● Salerno

● Taranto

TYRRHENIAN SEA

Stromboli ○

Vulcano

Messina ●

● Reggio

● Palermo

3340 m
▲ *Mt Etna*

● Cagliari

SICILY

Catania ●

MEDITERRANEAN SEA

Kilometres
0   50   100   150   200   250

0   50   100   150
Miles

▶ The flag of Switzerland.
The Swiss capital is Bern
but Geneva is far more
famous. Many international
organizations, such as the
Red Cross, have their
headquarters in Geneva.

MALTA   ■ **Valetta**

Central Europe

Europe's two largest mountain ranges, the Alps and the Carpathians, tower over central Europe. The mountain peaks are covered with snow and the lower slopes are well-forested. In other areas, there are fertile lowlands for farming and wide open plains where herds of cattle and horses graze.

Czechoslovakia, Poland and Hungary have been *communist* countries since 1945. In communist countries, the government runs most factories and mines, and many farms. Potatoes, wheat and sugar-beet are important crops on the farms. But, since 1945, more and more Poles, Czechs, and Hungarians have been leaving their farms to work in mines and factories. Poland is a major world producer of coal.

The river Danube is an important waterway in this region. Barges carry goods along it to other countries in Europe, and beautiful cities, such as Vienna and Budapest, are on its banks.

Austria borders Hungary and Yugoslavia. It has important tourist and timber industries. Most Austrians live in towns. Vienna, the capital, is famous for its music. In the past many famous musicians, such as Beethoven and Mozart, have lived and composed music there.

▲ Budapest on the banks of the Danube is a major city of central Europe. It was once two towns – Buda and Pest.

▼ **Thousands of holidaymakers visit Austria every year to enjoy winter sports and the sparkling mountain air.**

▶ **A glassblower at work in a small Czech factory. Glassware from Czechoslovakia is sold all over the world.**

▼ **The Austrian flag. Austria was once the centre of a great empire. Many different groups of people live there. But the official language is German.**

▼ **Many Poles are Roman Catholics and attend church regularly.**

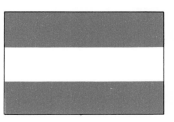

BALTIC SEA

U S S R

0   50   100   150   200 Kilometres

Miles 0   50   100

The flag of Poland

EAST
GERMANY

**The flag of
Czechoslovakia**

WEST
GERMANY

LIECHTENSTEIN

ITALY

Gdansk

Szczecin

Oder

Netze

Bydgoszcz

Vistula

Bug

Poznan

■ **Warsaw**

Warta

Neisse

POLAND

• Lodz

Wroclaw

• Lublin

Katowice

Krakow

Elbe

▲
1492m

Ostrava

Prague ■

Plzen

C a r p a t h i a n   M t s

CZECHOSLOVAKIA

Brno

Vltava

Vah

▲
2655m

Kosice

Danube

Linz

Vienna ■

Bratislava

Miskolc

AUSTRIA

Salzburg

Enns

Budapest ■

Debrecen

Inn

Innsbruck

Gross
Glockner
3797 m
▲

Graz

*Lake
Balaton*

Tisza

HUNGARY

ROMANIA

Szeged

Pecs

YUGOSLAVIA

*ADRIATIC
SEA*

39

Romania and the Balkan Countries

The Balkan countries are Bulgaria, Yugoslavia, Albania and Greece. Romania borders Bulgaria and Yugoslavia.

Greece consists of the mainland and over 1400 islands. It is very mountainous and sheep and goats graze over the hills. Only one-third of Greece is suitable for farming. But in spite of this nearly half of the people live on the land. Many farmers grow grapes for making wine. Sometimes the grapes are picked, left to dry in the hot sun, then sold as raisins, currants or sultanas.

Bulgaria, Yugoslavia, Albania and Romania are also very mountainous. But, unlike Greece, the mountains are covered with forests where wolves, wild boars and bears still live. Beneath the valuable forests there are rich deposits of copper, zinc, coal and oil. Many people work in industry turning these minerals into useful products. Many others, especially in Albania, work on farms in the valleys.

Yugoslavia and Greece have beautiful beaches and islands. Thousands of holiday-makers go there each year. Greece also has fascinating ruins from the times of the Ancient Greeks.

▲ High on the Acropolis above Athens, stands the Parthenon temple. It was built 2400 years ago.

▼ Romanian women rest before going back to their work in the fields of a large state farm.

▼ This man is weighing sacks of rose petals. Roses are grown in Bulgaria and used for making perfume.

▲ The flag of Romania. Many gypsies live in Romania and Bulgaria. Their language is called Romany.

▼ Two boys watch over a flock of sheep on the rough Albania hillside.

▲ The flag of Yugoslavia

▲ The flag of Greece.

Kilometres
0 50 100 150 200 250
0 50 100 150
Miles

USSR

HUNGARY

Mt Triglav
2863m
▲

Ljubljana

Drava

Zagreb

Tisa

Cluj

Iasi

Carpathian Mts

Timisoara

2543m
▲

Brasov

Galati

Sava

Transylvania Alps

2518m
▲

Turnu
Severin

ROMANIA

Ploesti

Belgrade

YUGOSLAVIA

Morava

Craiova

Bucharest

Sarajevo

Dinaric Alps

Danube

Ruse

Split

Nis

BLACK
SEA

▲2522m

Iskar

BULGARIA

Varna

Sofia

Balkan Mts

ADRIATIC
SEA

Dubrovnik

Burgas

2692m
▲

2496m
▲

Mt
Musala
2925m
▲

Maritsa

Rhodope Mts

Plovdiv

Skopje

Vardar

Tirana
■

2480m
▲

Thessaloniki

ALBANIA

2637m
▲

Pindus Mts

Mt Olympus
2917m
▲

LESVOS

TURKEY

GREECE

Delphi

AEGEAN
SEA

2376m
▲

Athens

Piraeus

Olympia

IONIAN SEA

Sparta

NAXOS

RHODES

MEDITERRANEAN SEA

CRETE

Iraklion

▲ **Barges wait to pass through locks at the Iron Gates near Turnu Severin, Romania. The Danube is an important waterway as it connects central Europe with western Europe and the Balkan countries.**

Union of Soviet Socialist Republics

The Union of Soviet Socialist Republics, the USSR, is the largest country in the world. It is more than twice the size of Canada, the second largest country and covers one-sixth of the world's total land surface.

Since the communist revolution in 1917, the USSR has developed from an old-fashioned farming country into a powerful industrial nation. It has large *resources* of coal, oil and natural gas. These provide fuel for the huge numbers of factories and industrial plants. The USSR, like the United States, has a large space industry. The first man and woman to be launched into space were Russians.

One-quarter of the USSR is farmland. Farmers work either on enormous state-owned farms or on smaller *collectives*. The USSR is a leading producer of wheat, meat and dairy products. The USSR is divided into 15 republics. These are made up of people of over 100 groups — Ukrainians, Uzbeks, Kazakhs and many others. Over 60 languages are used in the USSR. But Russian is spoken in most places because the Russian Federal Republic is the largest republic.

◀ **The flag of the USSR. Over 266 million people live in the Soviet Union and over half the working people are women.**

▼ **A young gymnast makes a spectacular leap. Soviet ice-skaters, gymnasts and dancers are famous all over the world for their skill and grace.**

▶ **In the USSR the distance from west to east is vast. When it is eight o'clock in the morning in the west, it is six o'clock in the evening in the east.**

▼ **Most people live west of the Ural Mountains. Here there are huge farms and cities. Farther east over the mountains there are high plains and vast forests. The Trans-Siberian Railway runs from Moscow in the west to Vladivostok in the east — over 9000 kilometres.**

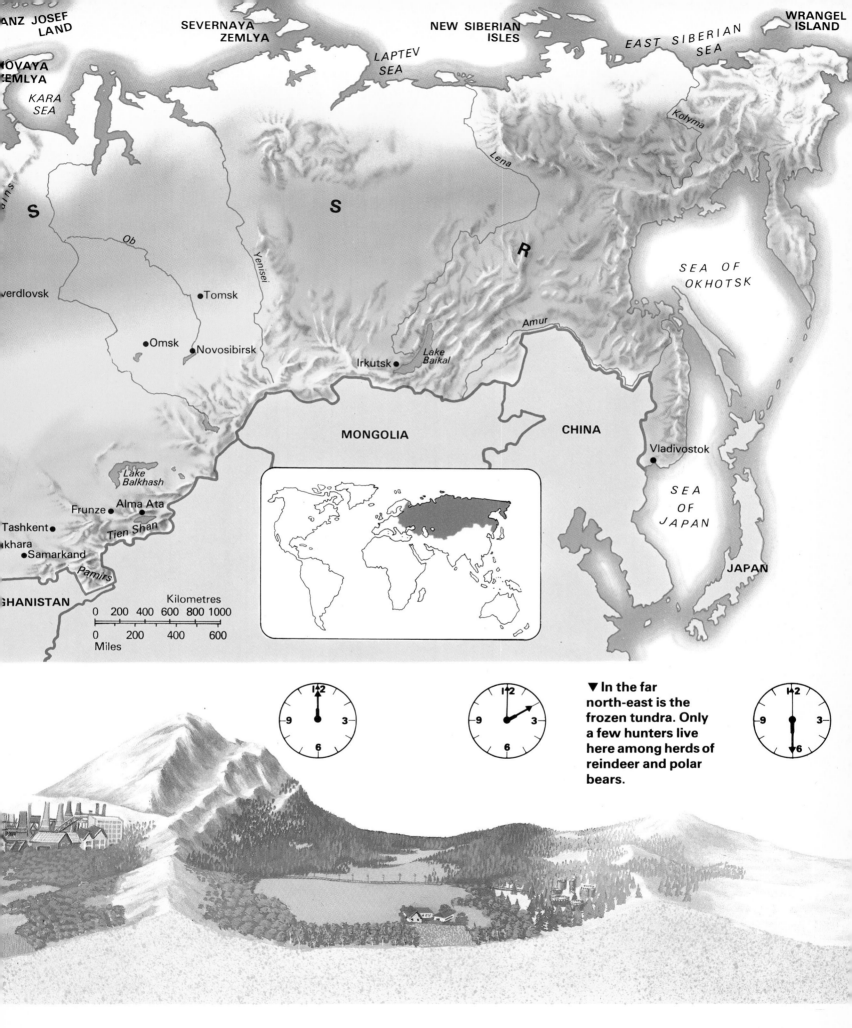

FRANZ JOSEF LAND

NOVAYA ZEMLYA

KARA SEA

SEVERNAYA ZEMLYA

LAPTEV SEA

NEW SIBERIAN ISLES

EAST SIBERIAN SEA

WRANGEL ISLAND

Kolyma

Lena

S

S

R

SEA OF OKHOTSK

Ob

Yenisei

erdlovsk

●Tomsk

●Omsk ●Novosibirsk

Irkutsk ● Lake Baikal

Amur

MONGOLIA

CHINA

Vladivostok ●

SEA OF JAPAN

Lake Balkhash

Frunze ● ● Alma Ata

Tashkent ●

khara Tien Shan

● Samarkand

Pamirs

GHANISTAN

Kilometres
0 200 400 600 800 1000

0 200 400 600
Miles

JAPAN

▼ In the far north-east is the frozen tundra. Only a few hunters live here among herds of reindeer and polar bears.

43

China

China is the third largest country in the world. It stretches from the plateau of Central Asia to the Pacific Ocean. There are more people in China than in any other nation in the world. Most people live in the fertile valleys of the Hwang Ho and Yangtze rivers and along the crowded coast. Since 1949, China has had a communist government. Mao Tse-tung was the leader of the government until his death in 1976. By encouraging everyone to put the needs of the community first, he helped turn China from a poor agricultural country into a great industrial one. Factories have been built all over China and many of the workers make iron and steel. But farming is still very important and about two-thirds of the people are farmers.

Look for Mongolia on the map opposite. Most of the country is desert and the few people living there are wandering herdsmen. Many of them live in tents. On the map you can also see the peninsula of Korea. It is divided into two countries – North Korea and South Korea.

▲ The flag of China. China is the oldest independent nation in the world. Its history stretches back for 2000 years. Taiwan, an island off the coast of China, is the home of Chinese people who are not communists.

▲ At the Temple of Heaven in Peking, emperors once made ritual sacrifices.

▶ The flag of North Korea.

▼ Light bulbs are made for export in this factory in Seoul, South Korea.

▲ A Chinese barge sails into Shanghai harbour. These boats are used by fishermen and merchants.

▼ In Mongolia there are probably two horses to every person! Most people are herdsmen.

▼ Hong Kong is a British colony on the coast of China. Its busy harbour seethes with activity.

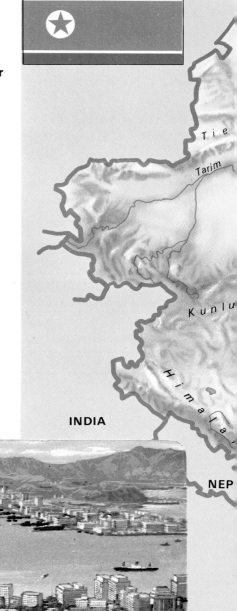

INDIA

NEP

▲ The Great Wall of China is more than 2400 kilometres long. It was built about 2500 years ago to keep out Mongol invaders.

Kilometres
0   200   400   600
0   100   200   300
Miles

USSR

MANCHURIA

Amur

Chichihaerh (Tsitsihar)

Harbin

Ulan Bator

MONGOLIA

Chilin (Kirin)

Hsi-Liao

Shenyang · Fushun

Anshan

NORTH KOREA

Gobi Desert

INNER MONGOLIA

Lop Nor

Paotou

Beijing (Peking) ■

Tangshan

Luta

Pyongyang

Altai Mts

Great Wall of China

Nan Shan

Tianjin (Tinsin)

Seoul

SOUTH KOREA

Altyn Tagh

Taiyuan

han

Jinan · Poshan

Pusan

han

Lanzhou

YELLOW SEA

Hwang Ho

Xian

CHINA

Salween

Yangtze Kiang

Nanjing

Shanghai

TIBET

Mekong

Chengdu

Wuhan

Hangzhou

EAST CHINA SEA

Tsang Po (Brahmaputra)

Lhasa

Nanchang

rest
48m

BHUTAN

Changsha

BANGLADESH

Guiyang

Fuzhou

Taipei

Kunming

TAIWAN

Si-Kiang

Guangzhou

MACAO · · HONG KONG

PACIFIC OCEAN

BURMA

VIETNAM

45

LAOS

SOUTH CHINA SEA

THAILAND

Japan

Japan consists of four main islands and about 3000 smaller ones. From one end of the main islands to the other, there runs a volcanic mountain chain. Many of the volcanoes are still active. Mount Fuji, the highest peak, is a volcano, but it has not erupted since 1707. Earthquakes are common in Japan. There are over 1000 each year, but most of them are only small tremors. There is not much land suitable for farming in Japan, because it is so mountainous. Rice is the main food crop on the little land which is cultivated. Fishing is important for it provides food for the large population. Japanese cooks use shark fins and eels to make soup and seaweed is also a favourite dish.

Japan is the wealthiest country in Asia, because it has an efficient manufacturing industry. Japanese workers make more cameras, televisions and ships than any other country in the world. There are many crowded industrial cities in Japan. But there are also peaceful temples and beautiful gardens.

▲ The red disc in the centre of the Japanese flag symbolizes the rising of the sun.

▲ Tokyo at night flashes with dazzling neon lights. It is the capital of Japan and one of the most crowded cities in the world. Almost 115 million people live in Japan.

▶ Japan's Hikari Express is the world's fastest passenger train.

▼ Kendo is a sport based on the ancient martial art of sword fighting. It is taught in schools along with judo.

▼ Thousands of calculators are made in this factory each week.

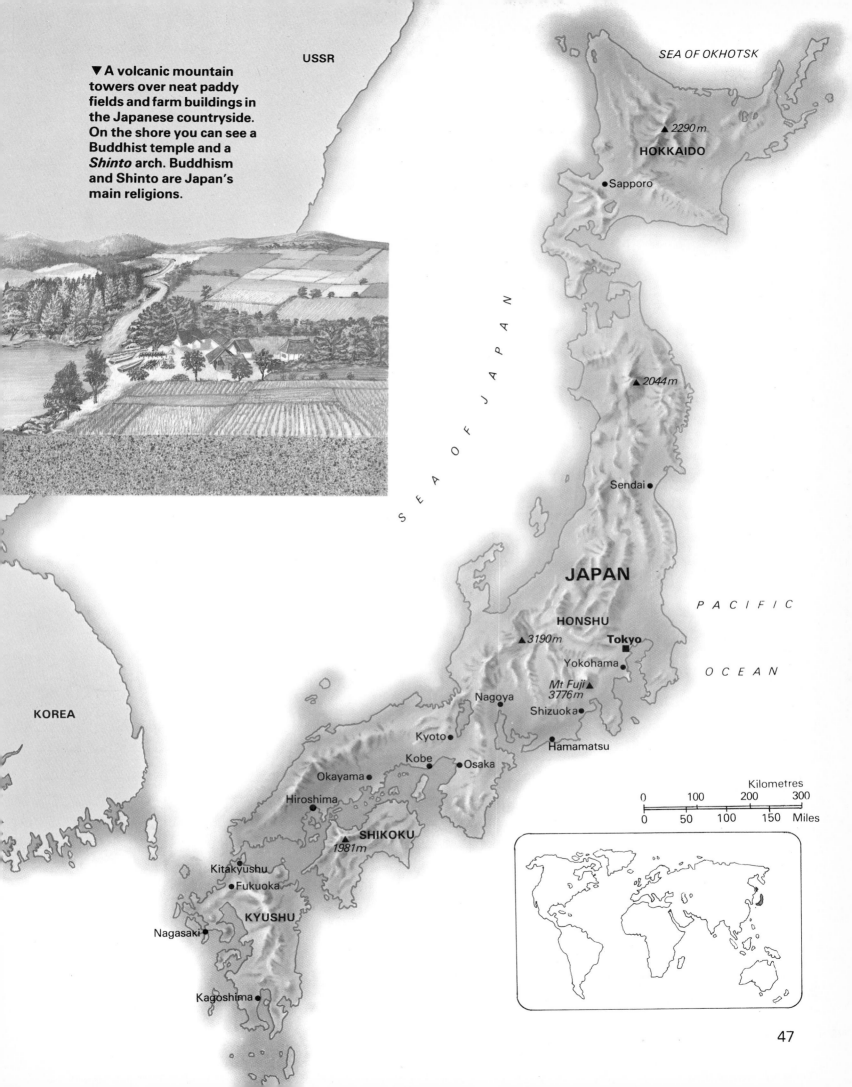

▼ A volcanic mountain towers over neat paddy fields and farm buildings in the Japanese countryside. On the shore you can see a Buddhist temple and a *Shinto* arch. Buddhism and Shinto are Japan's main religions.

USSR

SEA OF OKHOTSK

▲ 2290 m

HOKKAIDO

• Sapporo

S E A   O F   J A P A N

▲ 2044 m

Sendai •

JAPAN

HONSHU

▲ 3190 m

Tokyo ■

Yokohama •

PACIFIC

OCEAN

Mt Fuji ▲
3776 m

Nagoya •

Shizuoka •

Kyoto •

Hamamatsu •

KOREA

Kobe •

• Osaka

Okayama •

Hiroshima •

Kilometres

0   100   200   300

0   50   100   150   Miles

▲ **SHIKOKU**
1981 m

Kitakyushu •

• Fukuoka

KYUSHU

Nagasaki •

Kagoshima •

South-East Asia

Much of South-East Asia is made up of volcanic islands. Indonesia has over 3000 islands and the Philippines more than 7000. All the countries have a similar hot, wet climate and much of the land is mountainous.

South-East Asia is a heavily populated region. Many people live in stilt houses in fertile river valleys. Peasant farmers cut terraces into the hillsides where they grow rice, the main food crop. The slopes which are not tilled are covered in forest. There are also large rubber, coffee and tobacco plantations in Indonesia, Malaysia and Burma.

Mining is another important occupation in this region. Malaysia produces one-third of the world's supply of tin. It is one of the richest countries in South-East Asia. But many people in Vietnam and its neighbouring countries are very poor because of years of war.

Music, dance, drama and hand-made crafts keep alive the ancient stories and legends of South-East Asia. *Islam* and *Buddhism* are the main religions. Temple dancers tell the stories of their religion when they dance. The dance steps are very complicated and young girls begin to learn them when they are only five years old.

▲ In Burma, elephants work in the deep forests where there are few roads. They lift logs into the river and the logs float down to timber mills.

▼ The Indonesian flag. Indonesia has more active volcanoes than any other country. The Krakatoa eruption in 1883 was the greatest in modern times.

▲ This man on a rubber plantation is shaving off the bark of a rubber tree to let the latex run out. Rubber is made from latex.

▲ The flag of the Philippines. This country is the only Christian nation in Asia.

▲ The flag of Malaysia. Malay, Chinese and Indian people live in this country.

◀ The streets of Singapore are crowded with shops. The wealth of this tiny country comes from trading and manufacturing.

▶ Vegetables and fruit are paddled into the centre of Bangkok from the countryside. This capital city has many canals, called *klongs*.

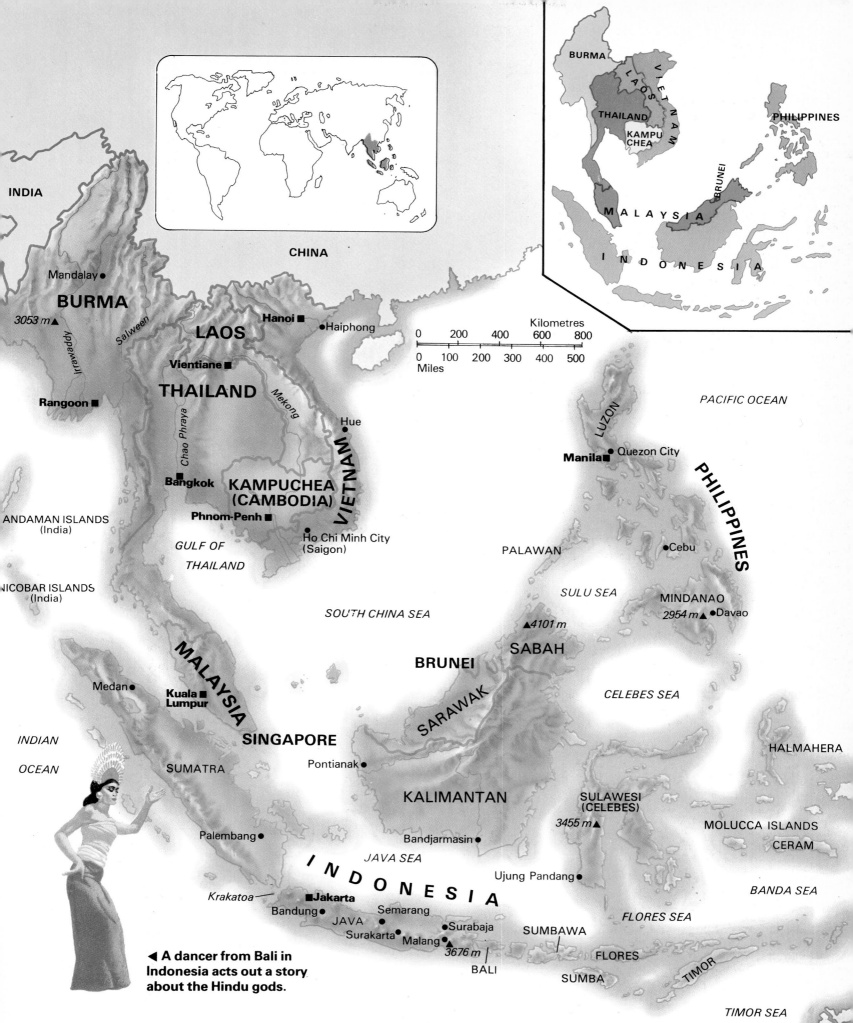

INDIA

CHINA

Mandalay ●

BURMA

3053 m ▲

Salween

Irrawaddy

LAOS

Hanoi ■ ● Haiphong

Vientiane ■

THAILAND

Mekong

Chao Phraya

Hue

Rangoon ■

Bangkok ■

**KAMPUCHEA
(CAMBODIA)**

Phnom-Penh ■

V I E T N A M

● Ho Chi Minh City
(Saigon)

ANDAMAN ISLANDS
(India)

*GULF OF
THAILAND*

NICOBAR ISLANDS
(India)

SOUTH CHINA SEA

	Kilometres	
0 200 400	600 800	
0 100 200 300	400 500	
Miles		

PACIFIC OCEAN

L U Z O N

Manila ■ ● Quezon City

P H I L I P P I N E S

PALAWAN

● Cebu

SULU SEA

MINDANAO

2954 m ▲ ● Davao

▲*4101 m*

SABAH

CELEBES SEA

BRUNEI

S A R A W A K

M A L A Y S I A

Medan ●

**Kuala
Lumpur** ■

SINGAPORE

*INDIAN

OCEAN*

SUMATRA

● Pontianak

KALIMANTAN

**SULAWESI
(CELEBES)**

3455 m ▲

HALMAHERA

MOLUCCA ISLANDS

CERAM

Palembang ●

● Bandjarmasin

JAVA SEA

Ujung Pandang ●

BANDA SEA

Krakatoa

I N D O N E S I A

■ **Jakarta**

Bandung ●

JAVA

Surakarta ●

● Semarang

● Malang

● Surabaja

3676 m

BALI

SUMBAWA

FLORES SEA

FLORES

TIMOR

SUMBA

TIMOR SEA

◀ **A dancer from Bali in
Indonesia acts out a story
about the Hindu gods.**

49

India and its Neighbours

This region contains the highest mountain range in the world – the Himalayas. It forms the boundary with Tibet and China and contains Mount Everest, the world's highest peak. On the map opposite you can trace the paths of three great rivers. They begin in the Himalayas and are the Ganges, the Indus and the Brahmaputra. India, Pakistan and Bangladesh are thickly populated nations. Farming is the main occupation, but there is never enough food for the huge numbers of people. Many children start to work in the fields with their parents when they are very young. Farming methods are often very simple because there is little money for machinery or fertilizers. The *monsoon* climate is also a problem. It means that twice a year there are huge downpours of rain. If the rain is too heavy, it washes away crops. If the rains come too late, the crops may die. The Indian, Pakistani and Bangladeshi governments are trying to set up more factories.

Religion is important in the everyday life of the people in this region. Most Indians are *Hindu* while most Pakistanis and Afghanis and many Bangladeshis are *Muslim*, followers of *Islam*.

▲ Every spring many Indians go to Varanasi to bathe in the holy water of the Ganges. The Hindus believe all life is sacred and do not eat meat.

▼ The flag of Pakistan

◄ Cinemas are very popular in India. More films are made in this country than anywhere else in the world.

▲ The Sherpas of Nepal live high in the Himalayas. They often work as guides on climbing expeditions.

▼ These women are planting out rice in Bangladesh. Each shoot is planted by hand in a flooded paddy field.

USSR

CHINA

Pamir Knot

Hindu Kush

JAMMU
&
KASHMIR

K2
8611m

Kabul ■

Khyber Pass

Srinagar ●

AFGHANISTAN

Islamabad ■

Rawalpindi ●

Kandahar ●

Helmand

IRAN

Amritsar

Faisalabad ●

Lahore ●

Karakoram Range

H I M A L A Y A S

Nanda Devi
▲ 7817m

Mt Everest, 8848m, is the
highest mountain in the world

▲ The flag of Afghanistan   ▲ The flag of India

PAKISTAN

Indus

Sutlej

Delhi ■

NEPAL

Katmandu ■

BHUTAN

Thar Desert

Jaipur ●

Agra ●

Lucknow ●

Mt Kanchenjunga
8598m

Darjeeling ●

Brahmaputra

Kanpur ●

Hyderabad ●

Karachi ●

Ganges

Allahabad ●

Varanasi ●

Patna ●

BANGLADESH

Ahmadabad ●

Indore ●

Narmada

ARABIAN SEA

Dacca ■

Chittagong ●

Calcutta ●

Surat ●

Nagpur ●

Mahanadi

BURMA

Bombay ●

INDIA

Poona ●

BAY OF BENGAL

Godavari

Hyderabad ●

Western Ghats

Krishna

Deccan

Eastern Ghats

Goa ●

▶ A fishing boat
from Sri Lanka.

Madras ●

Bangalore ●

▲ An engineer checks
equipment on an industrial
plant.

Cochin ●

Madurai ●

Trivandrum ●

SRI
LANKA

Colombo ■   ▲ 2524m

INDIAN OCEAN

51

The Middle East

Most people living in the Middle East are Arab. Their language is Arabic and their religion is Islam. Even in the non-Arab countries, Iran and Turkey, the people are Muslim. Many Christians live in Cyprus and Lebanon and most of the people in Israel are Jewish. The different religions of the people living in this area is the cause of constant trouble between them.

On the map you can see that most of this area is desert. Many of the people are farmers and the lack of rainfall is a serious problem.

On the Mediterranean coast, in river valleys and around *oases*, farms are irrigated with water from rivers and wells. But it is oil and not farming which has brought wealth to many countries in this area. Oil is the most valuable product in Iran, Saudi Arabia, Iraq, Bahrain, Kuwait and the United Arab Emirates.

Every year pilgrims arrive in the Middle East. Jerusalem, the capital of Israel, is regarded as a holy city by Jews, Christians and Muslims. Mecca and Medina in Saudi Arabia are Muslim holy cities.

◀ **The flag of Turkey. Four main languages are spoken in the Middle East – Turkish in Turkey, Persian in Iran, Hebrew in Israel and Arabic in all the other countries.**

▲ **Muslims worship their god, Allah, in mosques. This beautiful mosque is in Esfahan, Iran. Muslim women often cover themselves from head to toe in black robes.**

▶ **Fishermen in their boat on Lake Kinneret (Sea of Galilee) in Israel.**

◀ **A cotton-picking machine at work in Turkey. Some of this cotton will be woven into carpets.**

▼ **There are still nomads in the Middle East who wander over the sands with their herds. The oil is pumped through long pipelines to refineries and ports on the coast.**

Kilometres
0 50 100 150 200
0   50   100
Miles

BLACK SEA

Istanbul

Ankara

Izmir

TURKEY

Adana

Mt Ararat
5165 m

Tabriz

CASPIAN SEA

USSR

Halab
(Aleppo)

Mosul

Elburz Mts

Mashhad

CYPRUS Nicosia

SYRIA

Tehran

MEDITERRANEAN
SEA

LEBANON

Beirut

Damascus

Tigris

Mesopotamia

Baghdad

Great Salt
Desert

AFGHANISTAN

ISRAEL

Tel Aviv

Jerusalem

Amman

IRAQ

Euphrates

Zagros Mts

Esfahan

IRAN

JORDAN

The Dead Sea, 392m below the
average sea-level is the lowest
place on land

Basra

Abadan

Shiraz

Great Sand
Desert

PAKISTAN

EGYPT

NEUTRAL
TERRITORY

KUWAIT

PERSIAN GULF

BAHRAIN

RED SEA

Medina

Riyadh

QATAR

Dubai

Abu
Dhabi

OMAN

Muscat

SAUDI

UNITED ARAB
EMIRATES

ARABIA

Jidda

Mecca

Rub'al Khali (Empty Quarter)

OMAN

ARABIAN SEA

YEMEN A.R.

YEMEN P.D.R.

San'a

▲ The flag of Israel

Aden

GULF OF ADEN

53

Northern Africa

The Sahara covers almost all of northern Africa. It is the largest, hottest desert in the world, stretching for 4800 kilometres from the Atlantic Ocean to the Red Sea. In the north-west, in Morocco and Algeria, lie the rugged Atlas Mountains.

The people of northern Africa are mostly Muslim Arabs and Berbers who earn their living from farming. They live in river valleys and around oases, because there is no water in other areas. In Egypt it scarcely ever rains, except along the Mediterranean coast. Most farmers rely on the river Nile for water. The Aswan Dam, built on the Nile, stores water for use during dry periods. Tourists travel to Tunisia and Morocco to enjoy sunbathing on the beaches and wandering through the colourful bazaars. But many more tourists visit Egypt to see the pyramids at Giza — one of the wonders of the world.

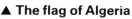

▲ **The flag of Algeria**

▲ **The flag of Egypt (above left)**

◀ **The flag of Morocco**

▼ **Children play in front of this unusual mosque at Mopti in Mali. It is built of mud on a wooden scaffolding. Mud walls last long in the hot dry climate.**

▼ **Below right: Egyptian farmers in the Nile valley grow food and cotton in small fields irrigated by ditches. Boats called dhows sail on the river.**

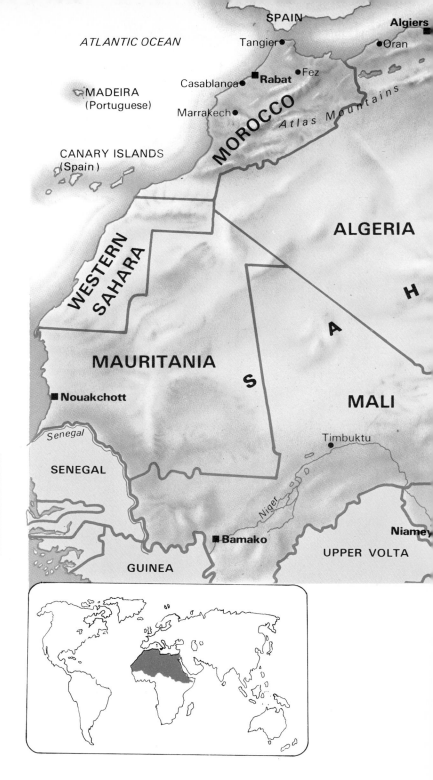

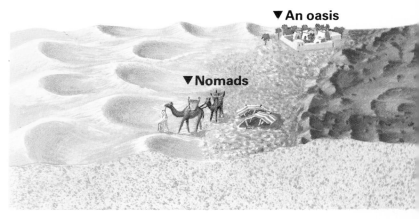

▼**An oasis**

▼**Nomads**

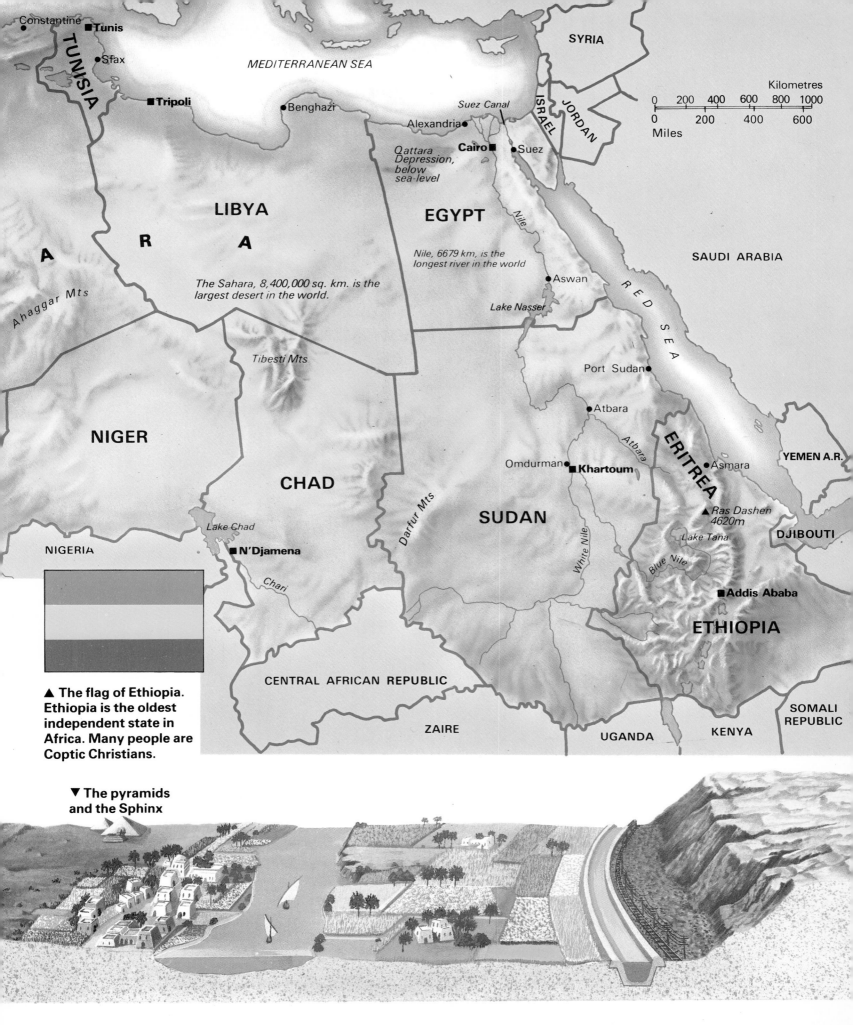

Constantine
Tunis
TUNISIA
Sfax

MEDITERRANEAN SEA

Tripoli
Benghazi

SYRIA

Suez Canal
ISRAEL
JORDAN
Alexandria
Cairo ■ Suez

Kilometres
0 200 400 600 800 1000
0   200   400   600
Miles

LIBYA

Qattara
Depression,
below
sea-level

EGYPT

A

R

A

Nile, 6679 km, is the
longest river in the world

Nile

SAUDI ARABIA

Ahaggar Mts

The Sahara, 8,400,000 sq. km. is the
largest desert in the world.

Aswan

Lake Nasser

R
E
D

S
E
A

Tibesti Mts

Port Sudan

NIGER

Atbara

Atbara

ERITREA

Asmara

YEMEN A.R.

CHAD

Omdurman ■ **Khartoum**

Darfur Mts

SUDAN

▲ Ras Dashen
4620m

Lake Tana

DJIBOUTI

Lake Chad

White Nile

Blue Nile

NIGERIA

■ **N'Djamena**

Chari

Addis Ababa ■

ETHIOPIA

The flag of Ethiopia.
Ethiopia is the oldest
independent state in
Africa. Many people are
Coptic Christians.

CENTRAL AFRICAN REPUBLIC

SOMALI
REPUBLIC

ZAIRE

UGANDA

KENYA

▲ The flag of Ethiopia.
Ethiopia is the oldest
independent state in
Africa. Many people are
Coptic Christians.

▼ The pyramids
and the Sphinx

Middle Africa

Middle Africa is a jigsaw puzzle of countries. Many different groups of Black Africans live there. Nigeria alone has 250 groups and Zaire has 200. The people speak many different African languages, including Swahili. But official languages are often English, French or Portuguese because most of these countries were once ruled by these European nations. The countries of middle Africa are going through many changes. There are new factories in Kenya, Nigeria and Senegal. Metals are mined in Zaire, Ghana and Sierra Leone, and oil is drilled in Nigeria. Coffee, cocoa, cotton and rubber are also grown on modern plantations. The money received from selling these products is used to build modern towns, schools and hospitals. But many of the people still live on the land in the same way as their families have lived for centuries. Some live in clearings in the hot forests and work small gardens. Others herd animals on the *savanna* grasslands inland.

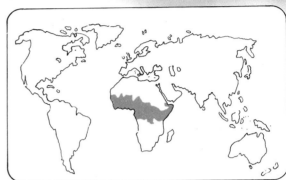

▲ The flag of Zaire

▼ A national game reserve in Tanzania. Mount Kilimanjaro, the highest peak in Africa is in the background.

▲ The flag of Nigeria

▶ A plantation worker in Ghana chops off the pods of a cacao tree with his machete knife. Cocoa and chocolate can be made from the seeds inside.

◀ The flag of Kenya

▼ People gather in this village market in Kenya to sell their hand-made goods.

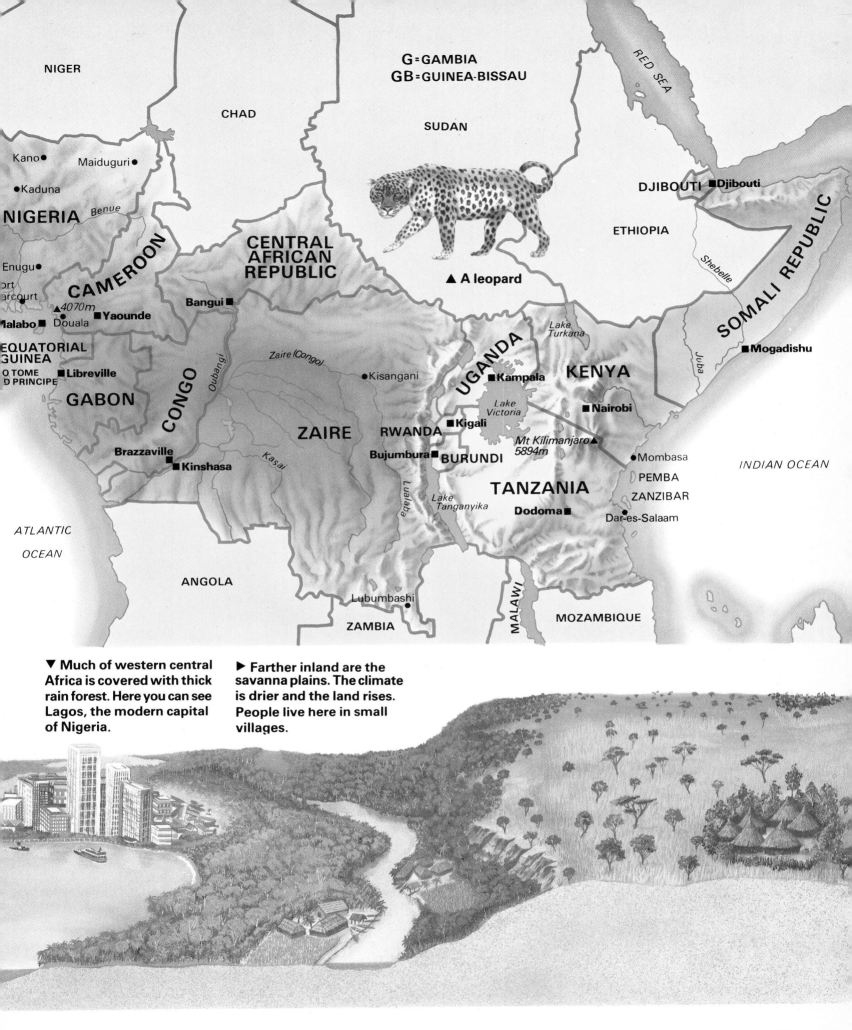

NIGER

CHAD

SUDAN

G=GAMBIA
GB=GUINEA-BISSAU

RED SEA

Kano●
Maiduguri●

●Kaduna

NIGERIA   *Benue*

CAMEROON

CENTRAL
AFRICAN
REPUBLIC

DJIBOUTI ■Djibouti

ETHIOPIA

SOMALI REPUBLIC

Enugu●
ort
arcourt

▲4070m

Malabo Douala ■Yaounde

Bangui ■

▲ A leopard

Shebelle

EQUATORIAL
GUINEA
O TOME
D PRINCIPE   ■Libreville

GABON

CONGO

Oubangi

Zaire (Congo)

●Kisangani

ZAIRE

UGANDA

Lake
Turkana

KENYA

Juba

■Mogadishu

■Kampala

●Nairobi

Brazzaville
■Kinshasa

Kasai

RWANDA

Bujumbura■

■Kigali

BURUNDI

Lake
Victoria

Mt Kilimanjaro▲
5894m

●Mombasa

INDIAN OCEAN

PEMBA

Lualaba

Lake
Tanganyika

TANZANIA

ZANZIBAR

Dodoma■

Dar-es-Salaam

ATLANTIC
OCEAN

ANGOLA

Lubumbashi●

MALAWI

MOZAMBIQUE

ZAMBIA

▼ **Much of western central Africa is covered with thick rain forest. Here you can see Lagos, the modern capital of Nigeria.**

▶ **Farther inland are the savanna plains. The climate is drier and the land rises. People live here in small villages.**

57

Southern Africa

Southern Africa is very different from the rest of Africa. To start with its climate is cooler than the rest of Africa. Look for the Namib and Kalahari deserts on the map. Unlike the almost barren Sahara, the Kalahari is a dry, bush-covered plateau.

Many Europeans also live in this part of Africa. Large numbers of them arrived in South Africa during the 1880s, attracted by the discovery of gold. Many stayed to farm or run mines and businesses.

South Africa and Zimbabwe are the richest countries in southern Africa. Men from poorer countries, such as Botswana and Lesotho, often go to work in their large manufacturing industries. South Africa produces a huge share of the world's gold and diamonds. In Zimbabwe, there are large cattle ranches and maize, cotton, and tobacco farms.

In South Africa there is a government policy called *apartheid* to keep Europeans and Black Africans apart. Europeans control the government and own the major businesses. Madagascar is one of the largest islands in the world. Most people are farmers.

▲ These South African miners are drilling deep into the rock in search of diamonds.

▼ Zulu women stop to talk during a festival. Zulus are the largest group of Black Africans in South Africa.

▲ The flag of South Africa   ▲ The flag of Zambia

▼ The Kariba dam on the Zimbabwe border provides water in the dry season.

▶ Fishermen return with their catch to the shore in Mozambique.

CONGO

ZAIRE

TANZANIA

•Cabinda

GOLA

•Luanda ■

Cuanza

ANGOLA

Benguela• •Lobito ▲ *2619 m*

Cuando

Cunene

Cubango

▲ **A giraffe**

Lake
Mweru

Lake
Bangweulu

COMOROS

Kitwe•

ZAMBIA

Lake
Nyasa
(Lake Malawi)

MALAWI

Lilongwe ■

MOZAMBIQUE

■**Lusaka**   *Zambezi*

Mocambique•

•Blantyre

Lake
Kariba

*Victoria
Falls*

Harare ■

ZIMBABWE

Beira•

INDIAN OCEAN

*Okavango
Swamps*

Namib Desert

NAMIBIA

•Bulawayo

BOTSWANA

WALVIS
BAY

Windhoek ■ ▲*2483 m*

Kalahari Desert

Limpopo

Gaborone ■

Pretoria

■**Maputo**

MOZAMBIQUE CHANNEL

Johannesburg•

Mbabane ■

ATLANTIC OCEAN

Kimberley•

Vaal

LESOTHO

SWAZILAND

Antananarivo ■

Orange

Bloemfontein• ▲*3482 m*

Maseru

•Durban

MADAGASCAR

SOUTH AFRICA

Drakensberg

■**Cape Town**   •Port Elizabeth

Cape of Good Hope

59

Kilometres

0   200   400   600

0   100   200   300

Miles

Canada

Canada is the second largest country in the world. Only the USSR is larger. Vast areas in the far north are uninhabited and only a small number of trappers and fishermen live in the snow-blanketed forests around the Hudson Bay. Most Canadians live in the south, not far from the USA border, where the climate is warmer. The Prairie Provinces of Manitoba, Saskatchewan and Alberta lie west of the Great Lakes. Sometimes they are called the 'food basket of the world' because wheat farms stretch as far as the eye can see.

Canada's original people arrived there over 20,000 years ago. They came from Asia and their descendants today are the *American Indians* and the *Eskimos*. British and French settlers did not arrive until the 17th century.

Large deposits of minerals as well as fertile plains and rich forests help make Canada one of the wealthiest countries in the world. Canadians are proud too, of their beautiful lakes and the cool, clean air of their forests.

▲ The red maple leaf in the centre of Canada's flag is the emblem of the country. Canada is divided into ten provinces and two territories.

◀ Logs for the timber industry are floated down rivers to sawmills.

▲ Today Eskimoes use power-driven sleighs called 'skidoos' to take them across the frozen land of northern Canada.

ARCTIC OCEAN

BANKS I.

BEAUFORT SEA

•Fairbanks

ALASKA (USA)

•Anchorage

Klondike•

YUKON TERRITORY

Great Bear Lake

▲Mt Logan 6050m

Yukon

Mackenzie Mountains

ROCKY

Mackenzie

Yellowknife

N

Juneau•

OCEAN

CANADA

BRITISH COLUMBIA

Mountains

ALBERTA

Edmonton•

Calgary•

VANCOUVER I.

•Vancouver

PACIFIC

U S A

QUEEN ELIZABETH ISLANDS

MELVILLE I.

DEVON I.

BAFFIN BAY

VICTORIA
ISLAND

BAFFIN ISLAND

ATLANTIC OCEAN

TH WEST TERRITORIES

HUDSON STRAIT

at Slave Lake

HUDSON BAY

Lake
Athabasca

NEWFOUNDLAND

Churchill

Nelson

SASKATCHEWAN

MANITOBA

QUEBEC

'atchewan

St John's

Saskatoon

Lake
Winnipeg

PRINCE
EDWARD I.

Regina

ONTARIO

St. Lawrence

Charlottetown

Winnipeg

Lake
Nipigon

NEW BRUNSWICK

NOVA SCOTIA

Lake Superior

Quebec

Halifax

Sudbury

Montreal

Lake Michigan

Ottawa

Lake Huron

Toronto

Lake
Ontario

Niagara Falls

Lake Erie

▲ A street sign in Quebec.
Canada has two official
languages – French and
English.

NORTH SHORE
AUTOROUTE
RIVE NORD

◄ Vast forests and
farmlands stretch across
Canada, from the Rocky
Mountains in the west to
the Great Lakes and cities
in the east.

Kilometres

0   200   400   600   800

0   100   200   300   400   500
Miles

61

United States of America

The United States of America, the USA, is the fourth largest country in the world and has the fourth largest population and land area. It is divided into 50 states and includes Alaska in the far north-west and Hawaii, a group of islands in the Pacific Ocean.

Like Canada, the USA was first settled by people whose ancestors came from Asia. In the 18th and 19th centuries, large numbers of settlers came to the 'New World' from Europe in search of a better way of life. Negroes were brought over from Africa to work on cotton and tobacco plantations. Today people from all over the world live in the USA.

Like their Canadian neighbours, most Americans have a high standard of living. The USA is an extremely wealthy country. It has large resources of oil, gas, coal and many metals, huge farms and plantations and more factories than any other country in the world.

▶ **Apollo 11 was launched from Cape Canaveral in Florida.**

▲ **The stars in the flag of the USA represent the 50 states which make up the country. The capital of the whole country is Washington D.C.**

▼ **The Navaho Indians are one of 200 Red Indian tribes in the USA. European settlers fought the Indians for their land and today most Indians live on reservations.**

For Alaska, see the map on p.60

▼ **The United States is so wide that it has several different time zones. When it is 7am in New York, it is 4am in San Francisco.**

CANADA

★ = state capital
N.H. = NEW HAMPSHIRE
MASS. = MASSACHUSETTS
CONN. = CONNECTICUT

NORTH DAKOTA
★ Bismarck

SOUTH DAKOTA
★ Pierre

MINNESOTA

Lake Superior

MICHIGAN

Lake Huron

MAINE
★ Augusta

VERMONT

N.H.

WISCONSIN

Minneapolis ●
St. Paul ★

Mississippi

Madison
Milwaukee ●

Lake Michigan

★ Lansing
Detroit ●

Lake Erie

Lake Ontario

Buffalo ●

NEW YORK

Albany ★

Boston ★ CAPE COD
MASS. ★ Hartford
CONN.
RHODE ISLAND

IOWA

Des Moines ★

Chicago ●

INDIANA

OHIO

Cleveland ●

New York City ●

NEBRASKA

Omaha ●

● Cheyenne

Lincoln ●

ILLINOIS

Springfield ★

Indianapolis ★

Columbus ●

Cincinnati ●

PENNSYLVANIA

Pittsburgh ●

Harrisburg ★

NEW JERSEY

Philadelphia ●

DELAWARE

● Denver

COLORADO

Arkansas

Topeka ★

KANSAS

Kansas City ●
St. Louis ●

Jefferson City ●

MISSOURI

Mississippi

Ohio

WEST VIRGINIA

Charleston ★

Baltimore ●
Washington DC ⊚

MARYLAND

VIRGINIA

Richmond ●

Frankfort ★

KENTUCKY

Appalachian

Raleigh ●

NORTH CAROLINA

Oklahoma City ★

OKLAHOMA

Red

ARKANSAS

Little Rock ★

Memphis ●

Nashville ★

TENNESSEE

Tennessee

Mountains

Columbia ●

SOUTH CAROLINA

Charleston ●

Atlanta ★

Birmingham ●

MISSISSIPPI

Jackson ★

ALABAMA

Montgomery ★

GEORGIA

Savannah ●

A T L A N T I C   O C E A N

TEXAS

● Dallas

LOUISIANA

Baton Rouge ★
● New Orleans

FLORIDA

Tallahassee ★

Austin ★
Houston ●

San Antonio ●

Rio Grande

GULF OF MEXICO

Tampa ●

Kilometres
0 100 200 300 400 500
Miles 0   100   200   300

Miami ●

63

Central America and the West Indies

The people living in Central America and the islands of the West Indies are descendants either of the original people or of Europeans and Negroes. Most of them speak Spanish, English, French or American Indian languages. In 1492, when Christopher Columbus reached the islands in the Caribbean Sea, he thought he had sailed around the world to India. He called the people living there 'Indians' and the islands were named the West Indies.

Central America and the thousands of West Indian islands are mostly hot and mountainous. The climate is ideal for growing fruit, coffee, cotton, tobacco and sugar-cane. Cuba is the largest of the West Indian islands and it is the third largest producer of sugar in the world. Many of the islands are popular holiday places for tourists because of their sunny climate and easy-going atmosphere.

In Mexico most people work on small farms. The main crop is maize. A favourite meal is *tortillas*, a type of pancake made from maize flour. Gold and other metals are mined in Mexico, but the most important industry is oil.

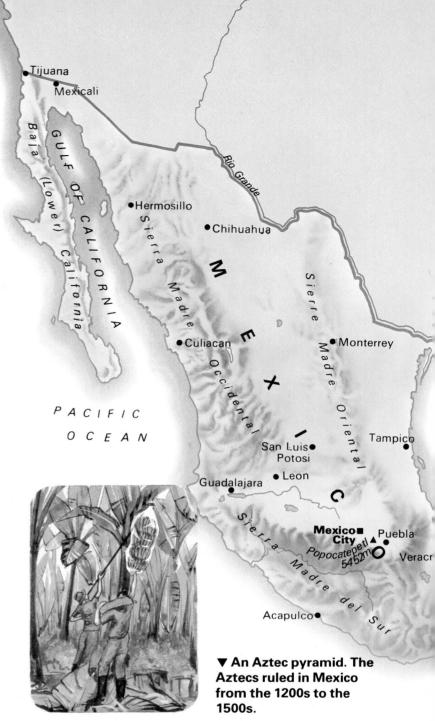

▲ The flag of Mexico. The capital of this country is Mexico City.

▶ Bananas grow easily in the hot, wet climate of Honduras and Guatemala.

▼ Women roll Havanas by hand in a cigar factory in Cuba. There are large tobacco and sugar plantations in Cuba.

▼ An Aztec pyramid. The Aztecs ruled in Mexico from the 1200s to the 1500s.

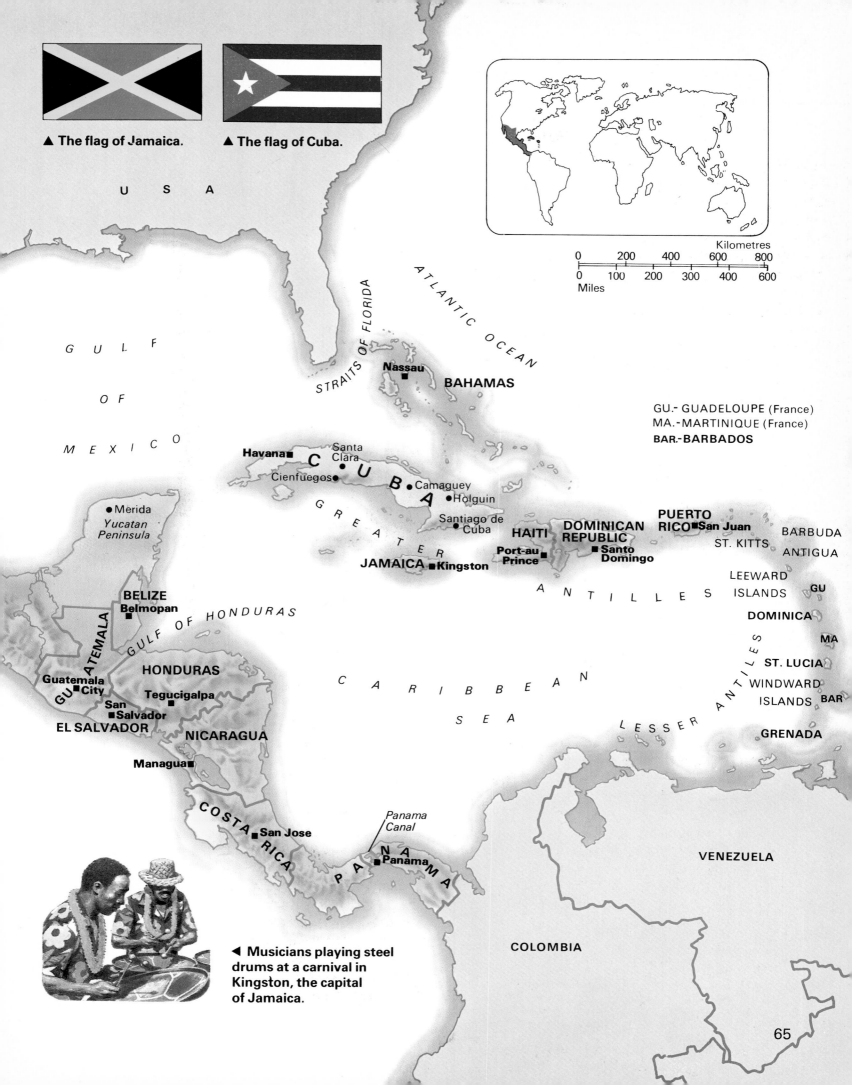

▲ The flag of Jamaica.

▲ The flag of Cuba.

GU.- GUADELOUPE (France)
MA.- MARTINIQUE (France)
BAR.- BARBADOS

U S A

GULF

OF

MEXICO

STRAITS OF FLORIDA

ATLANTIC OCEAN

Kilometres
0   200   400   600   800
0 100 200 300 400 600
Miles

Nassau

BAHAMAS

Havana   Santa Clara
C U B A
Cienfuegos   Camaguey
Holguin
GREATER   Santiago de Cuba

PUERTO RICO   San Juan   BARBUDA
ST. KITTS   ANTIGUA

HAITI   DOMINICAN REPUBLIC
Port-au-Prince   Santo Domingo

JAMAICA   Kingston

ANTILLES   LEEWARD ISLANDS   GU

DOMINICA   MA

Merida
Yucatan Peninsula

BELIZE
Belmopan

GULF OF HONDURAS

GUATEMALA

Guatemala City

San Salvador

EL SALVADOR

HONDURAS

Tegucigalpa

NICARAGUA

Managua

CARIBBEAN

SEA

LESSER ANTILLES

ST. LUCIA

WINDWARD ISLANDS   BAR

GRENADA

COSTA RICA
San Jose

Panama Canal

PANAMA
Panama

VENEZUELA

COLOMBIA

◄ Musicians playing steel drums at a carnival in Kingston, the capital of Jamaica.

65

Western South America

Look at the western part of South America on the map opposite. You will see a range of mountains running down the full length of the continent. These mountains are called the Andes. Communication between countries in South America is difficult because of the Andes. In the whole of Chile there are only six roads over the rugged mountains.

In the north the equator passes through Ecuador and Colombia. Bananas and coffee are grown on plantations in the hot, tropical climate. But much of the land is covered with thick forest and is unsuitable for farming. In the middle of western South America is the extremely dry Atacama Desert. Here workers mine copper and nitrate. The southern tip of Chile is cool because it is not very far from the frozen wastes of Antarctica. Many people in these countries live off the land, but farming is hard in most areas. Compared to the people of North America, the people of western South America are poor, especially the Indians living in the mountains of Peru and Ecuador. In Chile, people are leaving the farms to work in cities such as Santiago and Valparaiso.

▲ Indians in their colourful clothes gather in the market in La Paz to sell their vegetables. Over half the people in Bolivia are American Indian and speak the old Indian languages – Quechua and Aymara.

▶ Coffee is grown on large plantations in Colombia. The beans which produce the coffee are the seeds inside the berries.

▲ The flag of Chile

▲ The flag of Bolivia

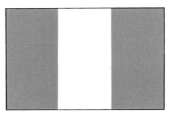

▲ The flag of Peru

▶ Most people in Peru live in cities on the coast. Others live on the high plateaux inland. In the high valley between the ranges of the Andes, you can see Lake Titicaca. Indians fish in the lake and farm the surrounding land.

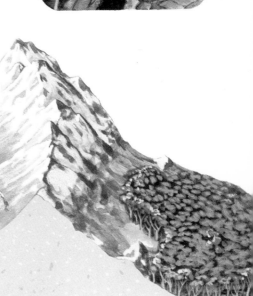

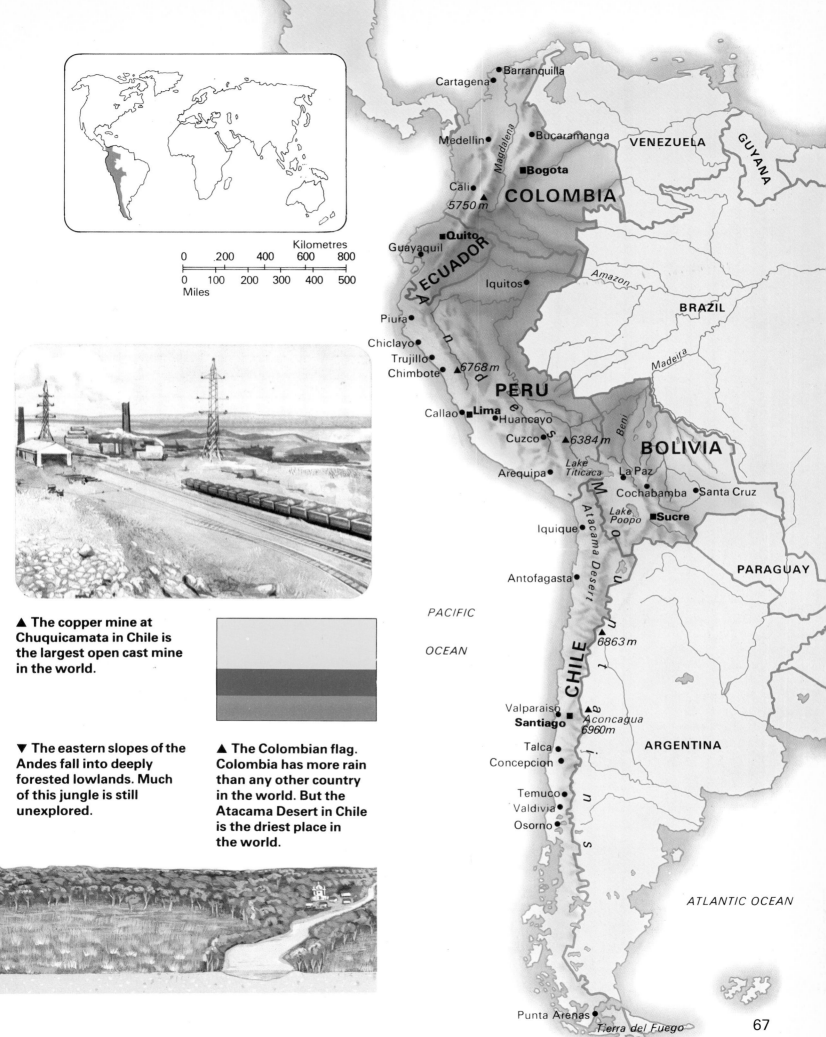

▲ The copper mine at Chuquicamata in Chile is the largest open cast mine in the world.

▼ The eastern slopes of the Andes fall into deeply forested lowlands. Much of this jungle is still unexplored.

▲ The Colombian flag. Colombia has more rain than any other country in the world. But the Atacama Desert in Chile is the driest place in the world.

Kilometres
0   200   400   600   800

Miles
0   100   200   300   400   500

Barranquilla
Cartagena
Medellin
Magdalena
Bucaramanga
VENEZUELA
GUYANA
■ Bogota
Cali
▲ 5750 m
COLOMBIA
■ Quito
Guayaquil
ECUADOR
Iquitos
Amazon
BRAZIL
Piura
Chiclayo
Trujillo
Chimbote   ▲ 6768 m
Madeira
PERU
Callao ● ■ Lima Huancayo
Cuzco ▲ 6384 m
Beni
BOLIVIA
Arequipa
Lake Titicaca
La Paz
Cochabamba ● Santa Cruz
Lake Poopo
■ Sucre
Iquique
Atacama Desert
PARAGUAY
Antofagasta
PACIFIC
OCEAN
▲ 6863 m
Valparaiso
Santiago ■ ▲ Aconcagua 6960m
Talca
Concepcion
ARGENTINA
Temuco
Valdivia
Osorno
CHILE
ATLANTIC OCEAN
Punta Arenas
Tierra del Fuego
Cape Horn

67

Eastern South America

People of many different races mix easily together in eastern South America. There are American Indians, *mestizos* who are mixed Indian and European people, and people who are direct descendants either of Europeans or Africans. Most of the early settlers were Spanish or Portuguese and most South Americans today speak one of these languages. Many people are also Roman Catholic.

The eastern part of South America is wealthier than the western part. Venezuela has valuable oil-fields. The money received from selling the oil provides Venezuelans with factories, modern homes and roads. Much of Brazil is covered in thick Amazon rain forest. Most Brazilians live in coastal cities, such as Rio de Janeiro and Sao Paulo and work in factories.

Argentina is the richest of all the South American countries. Farmers rear sheep and cattle and grow wheat, sugar-cane and cotton on the fertile *pampas*, or grasslands. Factory workers in the cities process these products.

▶ Oil wells in Lake Maracaibo, Venezuela.

▼ The huge statue of Christ looks over the beautiful harbour and lively city of Rio de Janeiro. A colourful carnival takes place in Rio every year.

◀ Gauchos are South American cowboys. They herd sheep and cattle on the pampas in Argentina and Uruguay.

◀ The Venezuelan flag. Angel Falls in Venezuela is the highest waterfall in the world.

▼ The Amazon River flows through thick, hot jungle. Groups of Indians live deep in the forest, cut off from the rest of the world. The Trans-Amazon Highway is being built through the forest.

TOBAGO
Port of Spain
TRINIDAD

Lake
Maracaibo **Caracas**

VENEZUELA

Orinoco

Angel Falls
Georgetown
GUYANA
SURINAM
Paramaribo
Cayenne
FRENCH GUIANA

COLOMBIA

Guiana Highlands

ATLANTIC OCEAN

Negro

Amazon

ECUADOR

Amazon
• **Manaus**
• **Belem**

• Fortaleza

A
n
d
e
s

PERU

Madeira

Tapajos

Xingu

Tocantins

Sao Francisco

Joao Pessoa
Recife
Maceio

PACIFIC OCEAN

*M a t o
G r o s s o*

BRAZIL

Brazilian Highlands

Salvador

BOLIVIA

Paraguay

• **Brasilia**
• Goiania

▼ The Argentinian flag.
Aconcagua in Argentina is
the highest peak in the
western hemisphere.

PARAGUAY

Parana

• Belo Horizonte

Rio de Janeiro
• **Sao Paulo**
Santos •
• Curitiba

M
o
u
n
t
a
i
n
s

Tucuman •

Salado

Asuncion

Parana

Uruguay

Porto Alegre •

ARGENTINA

San Juan •
Aconcagua 6960m ▲
• Mendoza

Cordoba •
Santa Fe •
Rosario •

URUGUAY

▲ The Brazilian flag. The
Amazon – the world's
greatest river system –
flows through Brazil.

Buenos Aires ■
■ **Montevideo**

C
h
i
l
e

Colorado
Bahia
Blanca •
• Mar del Plata

Negro

Kilometres
0   200   400   600   800

Miles 0 100 200 300 400 500

P a t a g o n i a

FALKLAND ISLANDS (BRITAIN)

Tierra del Fuego

Cape Horn

Australia

Australia is the largest island and smallest continent in the world. It is sometimes called 'Down Under' because it lies south of the equator among a group of islands in the Indian and Pacific Oceans.

Australia was discovered by Dutch sailors in the early 1600s. Much later in 1770, Captain Cook took possession of parts of eastern Australia for Britain. At that time the Aborigines were the only people living there. Later, in the 1850s gold was discovered and large numbers of settlers arrived from Europe in a hurry to make their fortunes. Today, besides gold, there are silver, copper, iron, zinc and aluminium mines.

Much of the west of Australia is desert. Most people live in cities along the cooler south-east coast. In the dry, central plains called the 'Outback', there are sheep and cattle stations. Sheep are kept mainly for their wool which is sold to several other countries.

▲ A surfer catches a wave as it rolls towards the beach. Australians are keen on all kinds of sport.

▲ The stars in the flag represent the six states of Australia. There are also two territories. The capital of Australia is Canberra. But each state also has its own capital. Only just over 14 million people live in Australia.

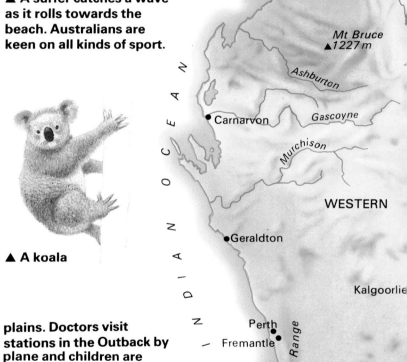

▲ A koala

▲ These women are sorting peaches in a canning factory. Many fruits are grown and canned in Australia.

▼ The Great Dividing Range lies inland from the east coast of Australia. Farther west before the desert, sheep graze on the

plains. Doctors visit stations in the Outback by plane and children are often given school lessons by radio.

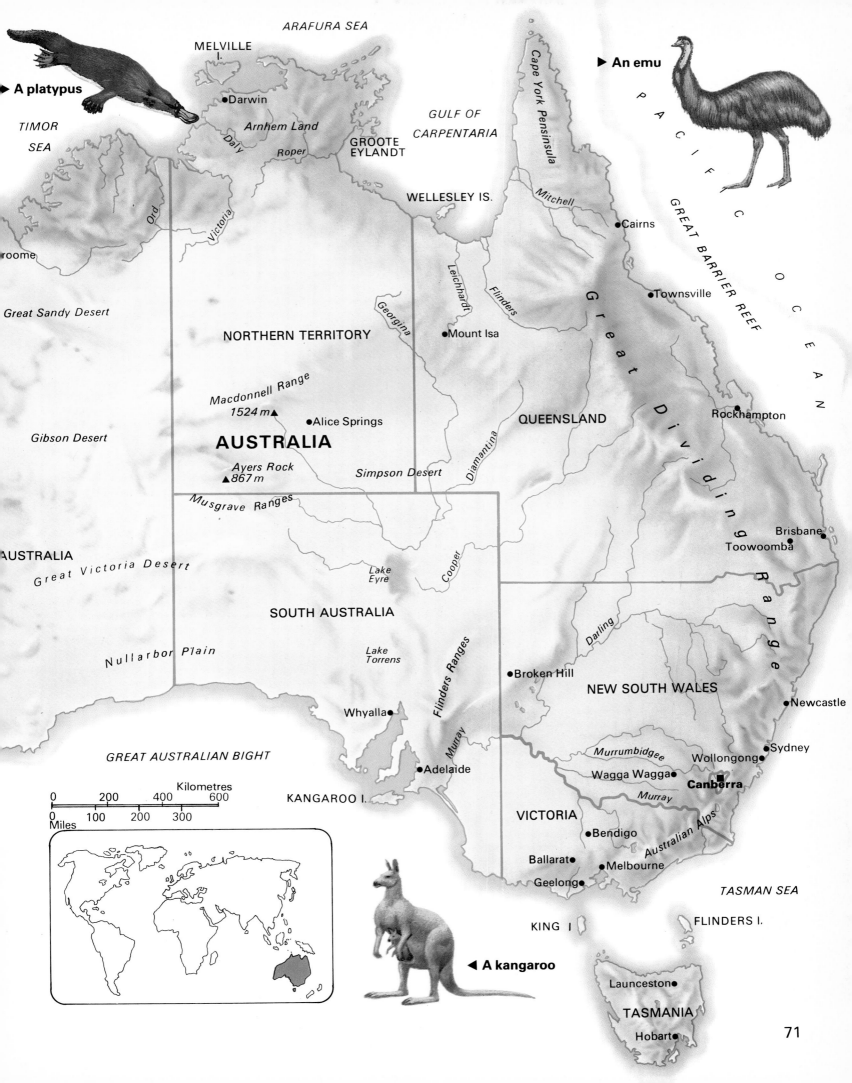

◀ A platypus

ARAFURA SEA

► An emu

MELVILLE I.

●Darwin

TIMOR SEA

Arnhem Land

GULF OF CARPENTARIA

GROOTE EYLANDT

Daly

Roper

Ord

Victoria

WELLESLEY IS.

Cape York Pensinsula

Mitchell

●Cairns

P A C I F I C   O C E A N

roome

Great Sandy Desert

NORTHERN TERRITORY

Georgina

Leichhardt

Flinders

●Mount Isa

GREAT BARRIER REEF

●Townsville

Gibson Desert

Macdonnell Range
1524 m▲

●Alice Springs

AUSTRALIA

Ayers Rock
▲867 m

Simpson Desert

Diamantina

QUEENSLAND

G r e a t   D i v i d i n g   R a n g e

●Rockhampton

Musgrave Ranges

AUSTRALIA

Great Victoria Desert

Cooper

Lake Eyre

SOUTH AUSTRALIA

●Brisbane

Toowoomba

Nullarbor Plain

Lake Torrens

Flinders Ranges

Darling

●Broken Hill

NEW SOUTH WALES

●Newcastle

Whyalla●

Murray

Murrumbidgee

Wollongong●

●Sydney

Wagga Wagga●

●**Canberra**

GREAT AUSTRALIAN BIGHT

●Adelaide

KANGAROO I.

Murray

VICTORIA

Australian Alps

Kilometres

0   200   400   600

0   100   200   300
Miles

●Bendigo

Ballarat●

●Melbourne

Geelong●

TASMAN SEA

KING I

FLINDERS I.

◀ A kangaroo

Launceston●

TASMANIA

Hobart●

71

New Zealand and the Pacific Islands

New Zealand and the islands of the Pacific Ocean are divided into three groups – Melanesia, Micronesia and Polynesia – according to the type of people who live on the islands. Kiribati and the Caroline islands form part of Micronesia, but Fiji and Papua New Guinea are included in Melanesia.

New Zealand is part of Polynesia because the Maoris, the original inhabitants, are Polynesian people. In the 1800s, settlers arrived from Britain to farm and to prospect for gold. Today most people live in towns and cities but New Zealand remains a rich farming country. Dairy farming is very important and there are over 9 million cattle and 55 million sheep. Many factory workers process meat, butter, cheese and milk.

Life on the Pacific Islands is often relaxed and simple. Many islanders live in small villages. They grow food in gardens and fish skilfully from canoes. Others on larger islands work on banana and cocoa plantations or mine phosphate, copper and other minerals.

▲ This hot spring at Wairakei in the North Island, is used for making electricity. New Zealand has many springs and geysers. Geysers spurt out jets of hot water and steam at irregular intervals.

MARIANA ISLANDS (U.S.A.)

CAROLINE ISLANDS (U.S.A.)

IRIAN JAYA (INDONESIA) PAPUA NEW GUINEA

Port Moresby

Coral Sea

AUSTRALIA

▲ Houses in the Fiji Islands are often built from the trunks and leaves of coconut palm trees.

▼ Experienced sheep-shearers can clip the wool from a sheep in less than 30 seconds.

▲ The flag of Papua New Guinea. The capital of Papua New Guinea is Port Moresby.

▲ The flag of New Zealand. Wellington on the North Island is the capital.

▶ Some of the islands in the Pacific Ocean have been made by volcanoes and are mountainous. Others are flat and made of coral. These islands are called atolls. Many islands are ringed by coral reefs.

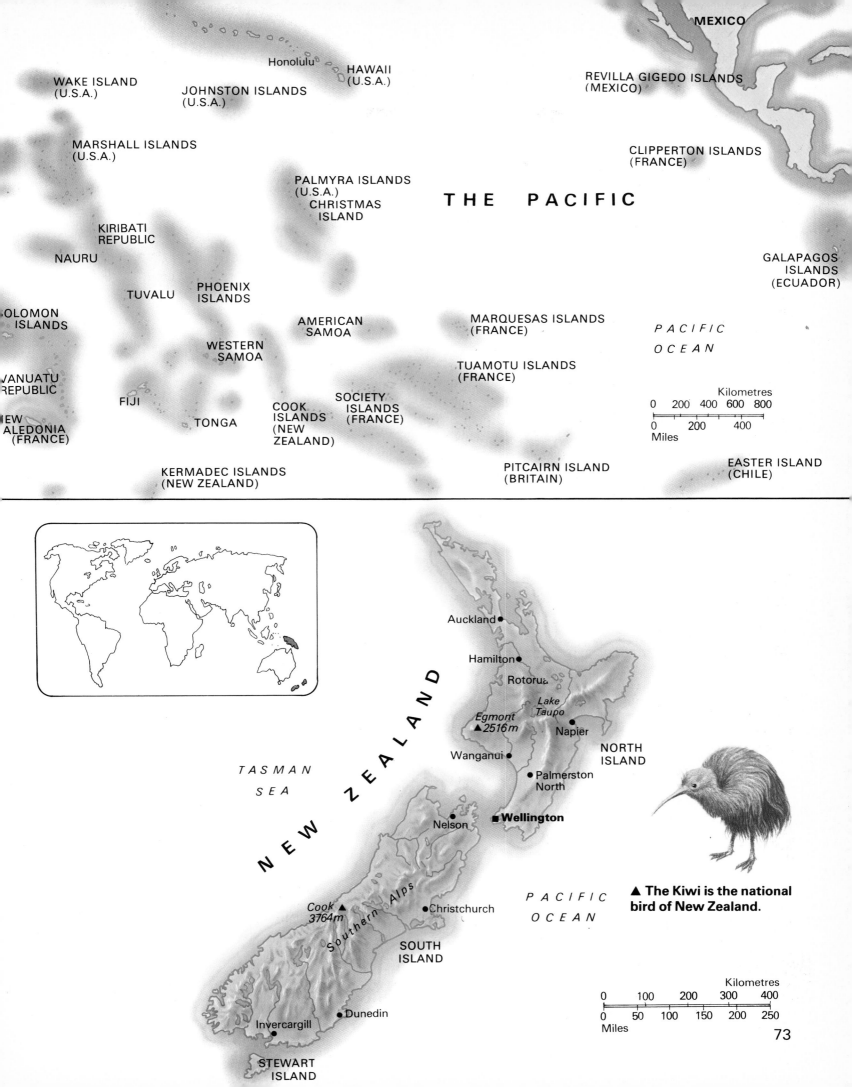

WAKE ISLAND
(U.S.A.)

Honolulu HAWAII
(U.S.A.)

JOHNSTON ISLANDS
(U.S.A.)

MEXICO

REVILLA GIGEDO ISLANDS
(MEXICO)

MARSHALL ISLANDS
(U.S.A.)

CLIPPERTON ISLANDS
(FRANCE)

PALMYRA ISLANDS
(U.S.A.)
CHRISTMAS
ISLAND

THE PACIFIC

KIRIBATI
REPUBLIC

NAURU

GALAPAGOS
ISLANDS
(ECUADOR)

TUVALU

PHOENIX
ISLANDS

MARQUESAS ISLANDS
(FRANCE)

PACIFIC

OCEAN

OLOMON
ISLANDS

AMERICAN
SAMOA

WESTERN
SAMOA

TUAMOTU ISLANDS
(FRANCE)

VANUATU
REPUBLIC

FIJI

COOK
ISLANDS
(NEW
ZEALAND)

SOCIETY
ISLANDS
(FRANCE)

Kilometres

0 200 400 600 800

EW
ALEDONIA
(FRANCE)

TONGA

0   200   400
Miles

KERMADEC ISLANDS
(NEW ZEALAND)

PITCAIRN ISLAND
(BRITAIN)

EASTER ISLAND
(CHILE)

Auckland ●

Hamilton ●

Rotorua ●

Lake
Taupo

Egmont
▲2516m

Napier ●

NORTH
ISLAND

Wanganui ●

TASMAN

SEA

N
E
W

Z
E
A
L
A
N
D

● Palmerston
North

■ Wellington

Nelson ●

PACIFIC

OCEAN

▲ The Kiwi is the national
bird of New Zealand.

Cook ▲
3764m

Southern Alps

● Christchurch

SOUTH
ISLAND

Kilometres

0   100   200   300   400

0   50   100   150   200   250
Miles

● Dunedin

Invercargill ●

73

STEWART
ISLAND

The Polar Lands

The Arctic

The area around the North Pole is called the Arctic. Much of it consists of the icy Arctic Ocean. But there are islands, including Greenland. Parts of North America, Europe and Asia also stretch beyond the *Arctic Circle.* The waters around the North Pole are frozen all the year round. But in other parts of the Arctic, the snow melts during the short summer weeks and patches of moss, lichen and bright flowers appear. These areas are the Arctic *tundra.*

Eskimos are the only people living permanently in the Arctic. Most Eskimos live on the south-west coast of Greenland and are skilled hunters and fishermen.

▶ **Most Lapps are nomadic herdsmen. In winter they live in the northern forests of Norway, Sweden and Finland. In summer they take their reindeer to graze inside the Arctic Circle.**

PACIFIC OCEAN

ALASKA (USA)

BERING STRAIT

EAST SIBERIAN SEA

BEAUFORT SEA

NEW SIBERIAN ISLANDS

LAPTEV SEA

BANKS ISLAND

CANADA

VICTORIA I.

QUEEN ELIZABETH ISLANDS

ARCTIC OCEAN

NORTH POLE

USSR

ELLESMERE ISLAND

HUDSON BAY

BAFFIN ISLAND

Thule

FRANZ JOSEF LAND

NOVAYA ZEMLYA

BAFFIN BAY

BARENTS SEA

SVALBARD (NORWAY)

▼ **An Eskimo in a kayak**

GREENLAND (DENMARK)

GREENLAND SEA

•Godthaab

•Murmansk

Tromso

LAPLAND

ARCTIC CIRCLE

ATLANTIC OCEAN

Reykjavik ■ ICELAND

NORWAY

SWEDEN

FINLAND

▲ **Polar bear**

▲ **Walrus**

Antarctica

The continent of Antarctica covers more than 13 million square kilometres. It is larger than Europe and contains over 90 per cent of the world's ice and snow. It is so bitterly cold in Antarctica that no one has ever lived there permanently. Whalers went there in the 19th century, but they never left the safety of their ships. Since 1911, when the South Pole was reached for the first time by Roald Amundsen, many scientists have been to the continent. They study the weather and the structure of the rocks buried in the ice. Research stations have been built there by a few countries, including the USA and the USSR.

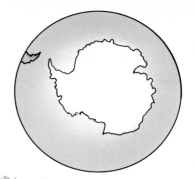

▼ In the summer, ships break their way through the ice floes to bring supplies to research stations.

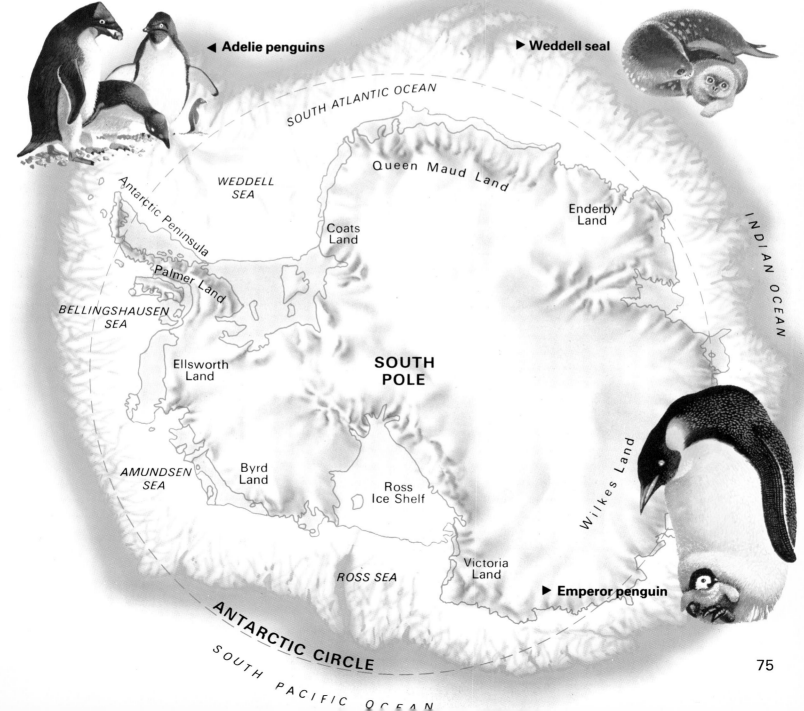

◄ Adelie penguins

► Weddell seal

SOUTH ATLANTIC OCEAN

WEDDELL SEA

Antarctic Peninsula

Palmer Land

BELLINGSHAUSEN SEA

Queen Maud Land

Coats Land

Enderby Land

INDIAN OCEAN

Ellsworth Land

SOUTH POLE

AMUNDSEN SEA

Byrd Land

Ross Ice Shelf

Wilkes Land

Victoria Land

ROSS SEA

► Emperor penguin

ANTARCTIC CIRCLE

SOUTH PACIFIC OCEAN

Riches from the Ground

Under the ground lie hidden riches in the form of rocks and minerals. Rocks are usually mixtures of minerals. Some are soft and others are hard. Metals are minerals that come from rocks that are called *ores*. Precious stones, such as diamonds, are also minerals. Other substances we get from the ground include coal, gas and oil which we burn as fuel.

To reach these riches from the ground, we must dig and drill into the Earth. Building stone and sand are dug out of big holes called *quarries*. Coal and many minerals are often mined by tunnelling underground. Oil and gas are drilled from underground pools deep beneath the surface of the Earth.

Huge oil rigs like this one are used for drilling oil under the North Sea. Storms can make the work difficult and dangerous.

These men are cutting out a block of marble in a quarry.

This man is operating a machine which digs out coal in underground seams.

Some Useful Minerals

Many of the things we use, including metals, come from minerals. To obtain metal, the ore is purified, usually by heating. Pictured here are four minerals with an example of their use.

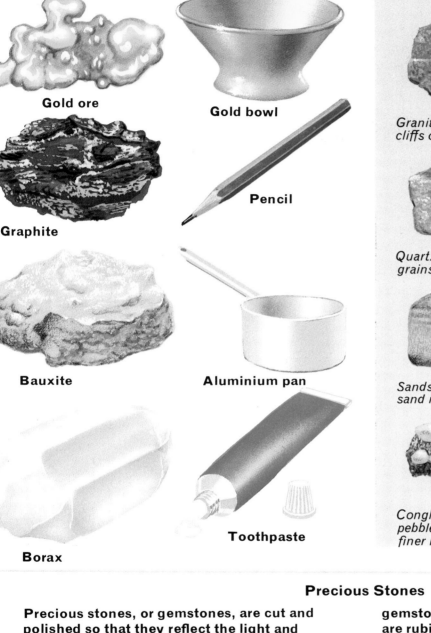

Gold ore

Gold bowl

Graphite

Pencil

Bauxite

Aluminium pan

Borax

Toothpaste

Rock Collecting

Collecting rocks can tell you much about the Earth and how it was formed. Some rocks have lovely colours and patterns, too. Here are pictured just eight of the many kinds of rocks you can find.

Granite, found on exposed cliffs or hills, is very old.

Obsidian, also called volcanic glass.

Quartzite formed of sand grains pressed together.

Slate is usually dark; it splits into flat sheets.

Sandstone, formed from sand in rivers and seas.

Flint, often found on chalk downs.

Conglomerate consists of pebbles cemented in finer material.

Limestone forms chalky cliffs. Underground caves occur in limestone.

Precious Stones

Precious stones, or gemstones, are cut and polished so that they reflect the light and sparkle brilliantly. The rarest and hardest gemstone is the diamond. Other valued stones are rubies, emeralds and sapphires. Gemstones are measured by their weight in carats.

Emerald

Ruby

Amethyst

Aquamarine

Wood

Wood is one of the strongest building materials. It can be shaped, bent, nailed or glued easily. Some types of wood have very beautiful patterns and colours. They are used to make furniture and *veneers*. Veneers are thin slices of wood which are glued to the surface of less attractive types of wood. Many familiar things are made of wood. Newspapers are printed on paper made from wood pulp. Substances such as plastics and artificial rubber can be made by chemically treating wood.

Most of the wood used today is softwood. It comes from conifer trees, such as spruce and pine, which grow quickly. A hardwood tree, such as a walnut or an oak, may take 100 years to grow big enough to be used.

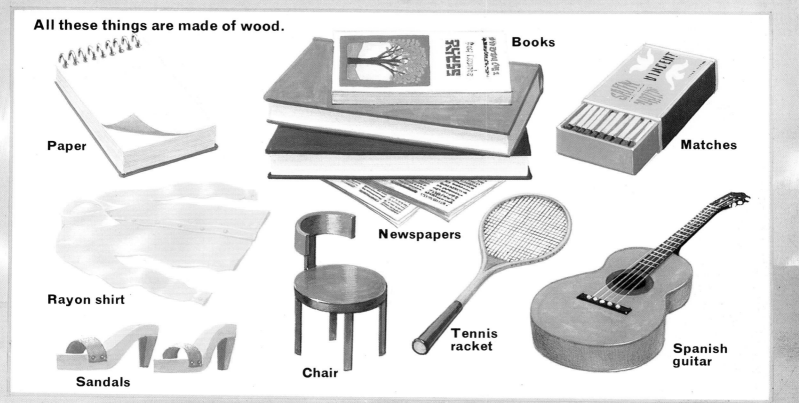

All these things are made of wood.

Paper

Books

Matches

Rayon shirt

Newspapers

Chair

Tennis racket

Spanish guitar

Sandals

The logging picture here shows some of the ways in which trees are turned into timber. First the lumberjacks, far left, fell the trees with machine saws and trim off the branches. The logs are taken by truck or floated down a river or dragged by chains to a sawmill. There the logs are stored in large ponds. Lumberjacks, below, sort them out and send them into the sawmill. Inside the logs are sawn and trimmed into planks. Then they are left outside in a yard to dry or season.

Textiles

Flax in flower

Flax field

Bactrian camel

Cotton flower and boll

Cotton field

Cocoons

Sheep

Silkmoth caterpillars

Our clothes, blankets, carpets, curtains, towels and other useful articles are made from woven threads or *textiles*. In the past all cloth came from plants or animals. These are the *natural fibres* – wool, cotton, linen and silk. Cotton comes from the fluffy seed or *boll* of the cotton plant. It grows best in warm countries such as Egypt and the southern states of North America. Linen is made from the stalks of the flax plant. One of the finest textiles is silk, which comes from the cocoon spun by the caterpillar of the silkmoth. Animals with thick hairy coats give us wool. Most wool comes from sheep but we also get wool from the camel and the South American alpaca. But, today many textiles are made by chemically treating substances such as wood, coal and oil. These textiles are called *synthetic*

fibres. You can follow how they are made in the box on the opposite page.

Cloth-making itself is a long job. The raw material has to go through many processes before it is ready to be dyed and woven into cloth. Often natural and synthetic fibres are mixed together to make the finished material strong, easy to wash, yet still soft.

Before there were factories, people made textiles at home. Some spun the fibres into long threads called *yarn*, while others wove or knitted it into cloth. For a long time now, however, these jobs have been done by machines in huge mills. The weaving machines or *looms* work at high speed and produce huge rolls of cloth. Big printing machines can then print colours, flowers and other designs onto the cloth.

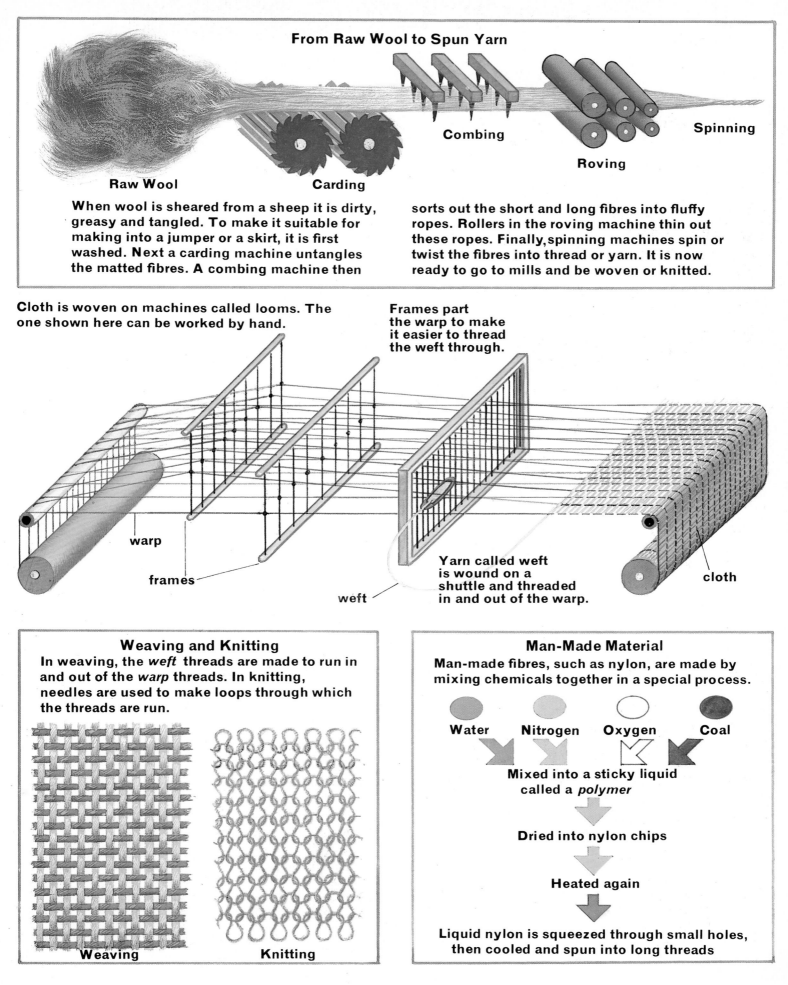

From Raw Wool to Spun Yarn

Raw Wool

Carding

Combing

Roving

Spinning

When wool is sheared from a sheep it is dirty, greasy and tangled. To make it suitable for making into a jumper or a skirt, it is first washed. Next a carding machine untangles the matted fibres. A combing machine then sorts out the short and long fibres into fluffy ropes. Rollers in the roving machine thin out these ropes. Finally, spinning machines spin or twist the fibres into thread or yarn. It is now ready to go to mills and be woven or knitted.

Cloth is woven on machines called looms. The one shown here can be worked by hand.

Frames part the warp to make it easier to thread the weft through.

warp

frames

Yarn called weft is wound on a shuttle and threaded in and out of the warp.

weft

cloth

Weaving and Knitting
In weaving, the *weft* threads are made to run in and out of the *warp* threads. In knitting, needles are used to make loops through which the threads are run.

Weaving

Knitting

Man-Made Material
Man-made fibres, such as nylon, are made by mixing chemicals together in a special process.

Water **Nitrogen** **Oxygen** **Coal**

Mixed into a sticky liquid called a *polymer*

Dried into nylon chips

Heated again

Liquid nylon is squeezed through small holes, then cooled and spun into long threads

Things We Eat

Only plants make their own food. Animals – including people – must eat plants or other animals to live. To keep our bodies healthy, we need several different kinds of foods. The food we get from animals, such as meat, milk, eggs and fish, gives us *proteins* or body-building chemicals, *fats*, and *minerals*, such as calcium. The food we get from plants, such as wheat, rice, fruit and sugar give us energy-making *carbohydrates* and sugars. Different foods contain substances called *vitamins*. For instance, oranges contain vitamin C. Our bodies need vitamins to keep fit and to grow properly.

You can see here some of the foods we eat and where they come from. Some foods can be eaten straightaway. Others must be treated in a factory. For instance, wheat is ground into flour and then baked into bread. Not everyone gets enough to eat. In parts of the world, people are lucky if they get a bowl of rice and a few vegetables every day. Providing food for the world's hungry people is one of our greatest problems today.

Some food comes from animals.

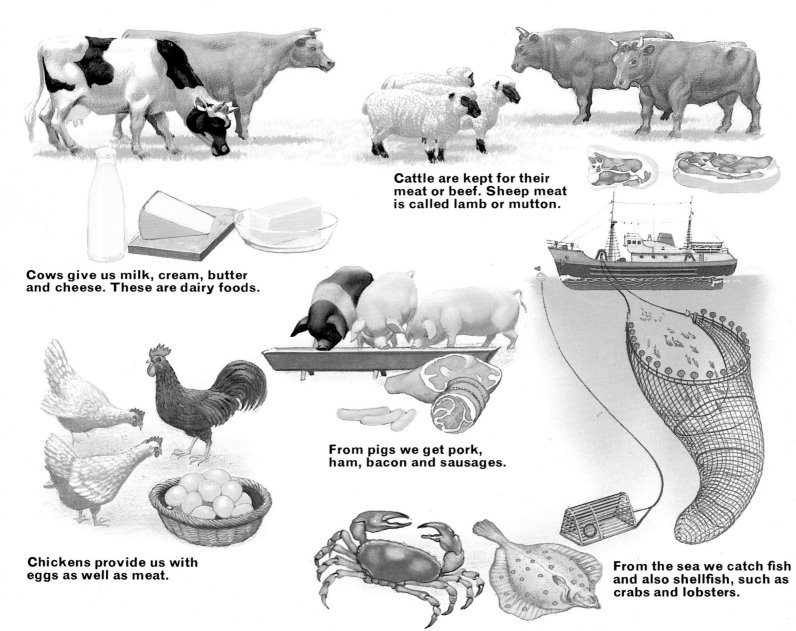

Cattle are kept for their meat or beef. Sheep meat is called lamb or mutton.

Cows give us milk, cream, butter and cheese. These are dairy foods.

From pigs we get pork, ham, bacon and sausages.

Chickens provide us with eggs as well as meat.

From the sea we catch fish and also shellfish, such as crabs and lobsters.

Tomatoes

Beans

Preserving food

It is useful to be able to keep food without it going bad. We can do this by drying it, freezing it, or boiling it inside cans. In a modern canning factory, most of the work is done by huge machines. Follow the picture and see how baked beans get into cans.

The beans are baked in ovens.

The beans and sauce are put into tins and sealed up.

The tins are heated to kill any germs.

Tomatoes and spices are mixed into a sauce.

Some food comes from plants.

A tea picker at work. Tea comes from the crushed leaves of the tea bush.

Chocolate is made from cacao beans found in the fruit of a South American tree.

From trees we get many delicious fruits – apples, pears, cherries, lemons, plums, oranges and bananas.

Sugar cane is grown in hot countries. The cane is crushed and purified to provide sugar.

Vegetables are grown all over the world in market gardens. There are many varieties and you can see some of them here.

From huge wheat fields like this comes the grain from which bread, cakes and pastries are made.

Rice is one of the world's most important crops. In Asia it is grown in flooded paddy fields.

83

What People Wear

There are many sorts of clothes in all kinds of colours and styles. Clothes keep us warm and dry. But people also choose clothes to make themselves look good.
The clothes people wear can also be a uniform and tell us what kind of work a person does. Many countries have a national costume. Sometimes people wear their national costume on special days. You can see some national costumes in the picture below.

Indian woman

Burmese man

Japanese woman

Mexican woman

Eskimo man

Arab woman

Ethiopian man

Spanish woman

Bolivian woman

Austrian man

Czech woman

Clothes have changed throughout history as different fashions became popular. Here are five European styles from different ages.

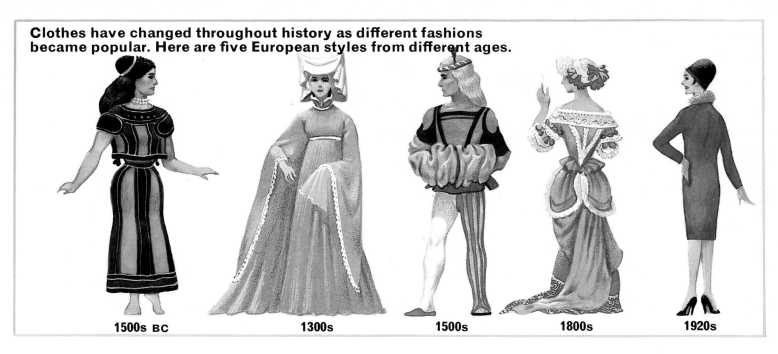

1500s BC **1300s** **1500s** **1800s** **1920s**

Some people wear special clothes to work

Ballet costume **Spacesuit** **Chef's hat and apron**

Diving suit **Nurse's uniform** **Clown's costume**

Disguise Yourself as a Clown

Sock *Wool yarn* *Soft crayon*

Cut *Face cream*

Cut off the foot of a large white sock. Tie a string around the cut end and turn it inside out. Glue or sew bits of yarn to this sock cap. Put it on and tuck in all your hair.

Cover your face and neck with face cream — ask someone for this. Pat onto it flour or talcum powder. With an old lipstick or soft crayons, draw in eyebrows, long eyelashes, a mouth and red cheeks. Dress up in old clothes, like the clown to the left.

Homes from Many Lands

The kind of home we live in depends on the kind of climate we have and the building materials we can use. The Bedouin tent is easy to carry about and good at keeping out the sun in the desert. The Swiss chalet has a sloping roof so that snow slides off it. A house on stilts is useful in a land where there are many floods. In cities there is very little land for building. Large numbers of people often live crowded together. Some people live on top of one another in tall apartment blocks.

Dutch town houses are built of brick.

In the Middle East the wandering Bedouin tribes live in tents.

Eskimoes once used to build homes called igloos from blocks of ice.

Swiss chalet

A stilt house in the Philippines.

Woven grass and branches make cool, movable homes in parts of Africa.

All over the world people live in boats. This one is in India.

Houses in North Africa have thick walls to keep them cool.

This old-style Australian ranch house has wide verandahs to keep the inside of the house cool.

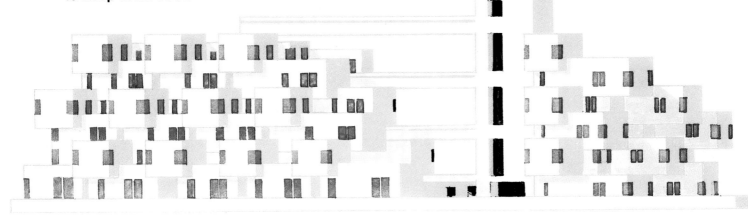

An apartment block, like this one in Canada, can house many people on a small piece of land.

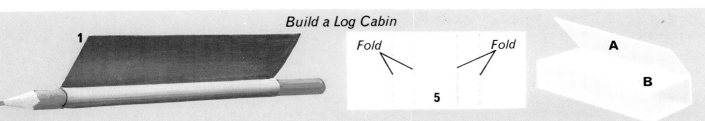

Build a Log Cabin

To make the logs, roll a sheet of paper around a pencil. Stick down the end of the paper with glue, 1. Pull out the pencil. Build the walls by glueing the logs on top of one another, 2. Cut logs smaller to make the peaks, 3, for the roof.

To make the chimney, fold a wide sheet of paper as in the picture 5. Glue A to B. Trim the roof on one side, 6, and glue the chimney into place.

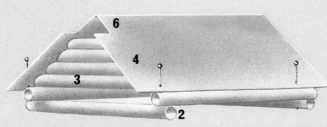

To make the roof, fold a large sheet of paper and stick pins in the corners to hold it in place, 4.

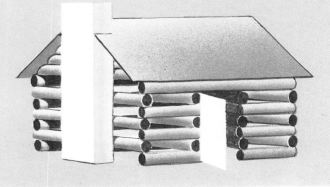

All Kinds of Buildings

There are many kinds of buildings around you – houses, shops, schools, offices, hospitals and factories. There may also be a famous building. Many famous buildings are very old. Some are castles and forts. Some were built as places to worship gods. Others are monuments, built to celebrate a person or something that happened. On this page you can see some very different buildings. Some are old and some are fairly new. They come from all over the world. In the past it took many years to finish an important building. Today, with modern machines and methods, builders work much faster.

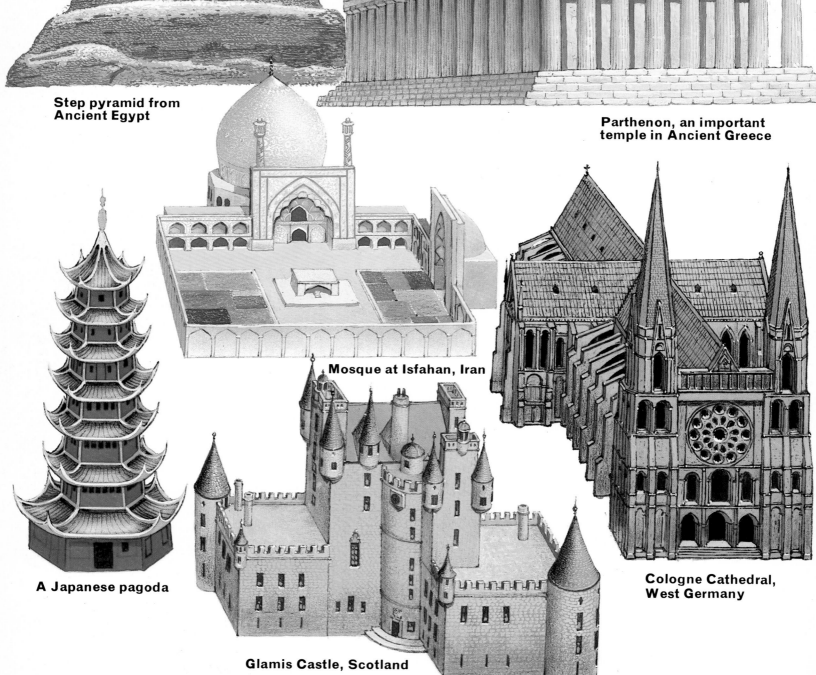

Step pyramid from Ancient Egypt

Parthenon, an important temple in Ancient Greece

Mosque at Isfahan, Iran

A Japanese pagoda

Glamis Castle, Scotland

Cologne Cathedral, West Germany

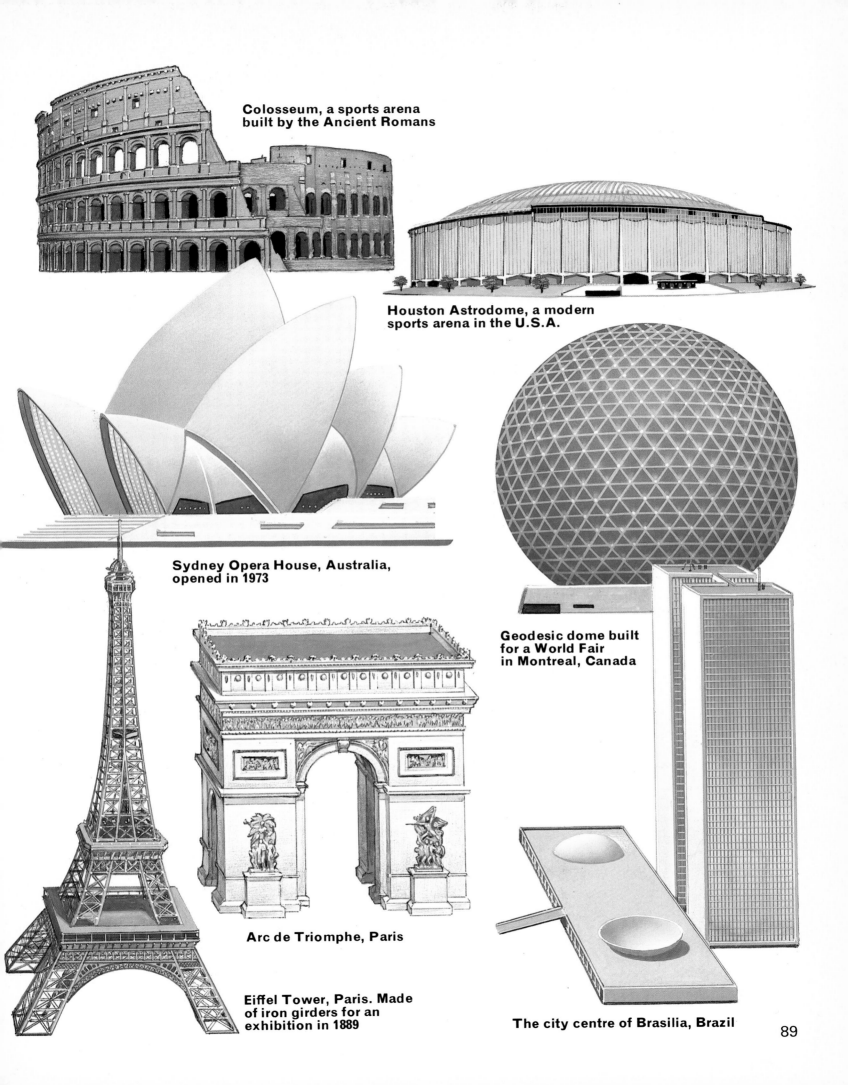

Colosseum, a sports arena
built by the Ancient Romans

Houston Astrodome, a modern
sports arena in the U.S.A.

Sydney Opera House, Australia,
opened in 1973

Geodesic dome built
for a World Fair
in Montreal, Canada

Arc de Triomphe, Paris

Eiffel Tower, Paris. Made
of iron girders for an
exhibition in 1889

The city centre of Brasilia, Brazil

People from the Past

Cro-Magnon people lived inside caves over 30,000 years ago. They hunted animals with spears. Deep inside their caves they painted pictures of horses, reindeer and bison.

Beside the River Nile arose a mighty empire – Ancient Egypt. The Ancient Egyptians buried their kings, called *pharaohs*, in tombs deep inside huge stone pyramids. Thousands of slaves worked for years to build these tombs.

The Ancient Chinese built the Great Wall of China to keep out raiding tribes. It stretches for about 2500 kilometres. The Chinese are great inventors and were the first to make paper and gunpowder.

Many thinkers and artists lived in Ancient Greece. Beautiful temples, such as the Acropolis shown below, were built to honour their gods. The Ancient Greeks also loved sport. They held the first Olympic Games.

Ancient Rome was a mighty empire. The Romans built solid roads and bridges and conquered many lands with their well-trained armies. Enemy forts were besieged with battering rams and wooden towers.

The Maya people lived in Central America. As part of their religion they sacrificed people from the top of great pyramid-shaped temples. They had a system of picture writing and a good calendar.

Explorers

The first explorers were the Ancient Greeks and Phoenicians. They sailed out from the Mediterranean Sea to explore the coast of Africa and went as far north as Britain. The Vikings were bold sailors and they probably discovered America about AD 1000.
In the 1200s Marco Polo journeyed from Venice in Italy across Asia to China. Until Columbus sailed to America in 1492, many people believed the world was flat. The first round-the-world voyage was made, in 1522, by Magellan's expedition. Soon European ships were trading with India and the East Indies. In the 1700s James Cook explored the huge Pacific Ocean and Australia. Africa was first crossed by Europeans in the 1800s. The last parts of the Earth to be explored were the Arctic and the Antarctic regions.

In 1492 Columbus sailed west from Spain, with three ships, the Santa Maria, the Niña and the Pinta. He was looking for a sea route to the East but instead discovered America.

Captain James Cook made three voyages to the Pacific between 1768 and 1779. He visited Tahiti, New Zealand and Australia. Cook was killed in Hawaii.

The Norwegian explorer Roald Amundsen won the race to the South Pole in 1911. Conditions were so harsh that the men had to eat most of their dogs on the way.

Inventors

Science and invention play a very important part in the way we live. Modern science began to develop long ago in the 1500s with the work of men like Copernicus and Galileo. They began to examine the world by means of *experiments*.

There have been many ages of discovery since this time and very many inventions which have changed the way people live. In the 1700s for example, the invention of the steam engine turned many farm workers into factory workers. This change is called the *Industrial Revolution*.

In the 1800s came railways and motor cars and in the 1900s wonder drugs, radio, television, aeroplanes and space travel. Today we are living through an Electronic Revolution and computers are changing our lives.

Galileo in 1609 was the first to examine the sky through a telescope. Others, like the professor in the picture, were too afraid to look through the new instrument.

At one time all books were written by hand. But in the 1440s Johann Gutenberg invented a printing press. This made it possible for more people to read books.

Louis Pasteur discovered the existence of germs and how to kill them. Today we drink pasteurized milk. This milk is treated by Pasteur's method to kill harmful germs.

Thomas Edison invented the phonograph in 1877. This was the first sound recorder and record player. He also invented the electric light bulb.

On the Road

The very first travellers had to carry or drag their belongings. Then they trained animals to carry loads and to drag sleds. Around 3500 BC the Ancient Sumerians began to use wheeled carts. From that time and for hundreds of years people travelled in various types of carriages pulled by animals.

For many years, however, there were no roads – only muddy tracks worn by feet or cart wheels. Yet today huge motorways run across countries. Cities are crowded with cars, trucks, buses and bicycles. In the picture you can follow the story of road travel and the making of roads.

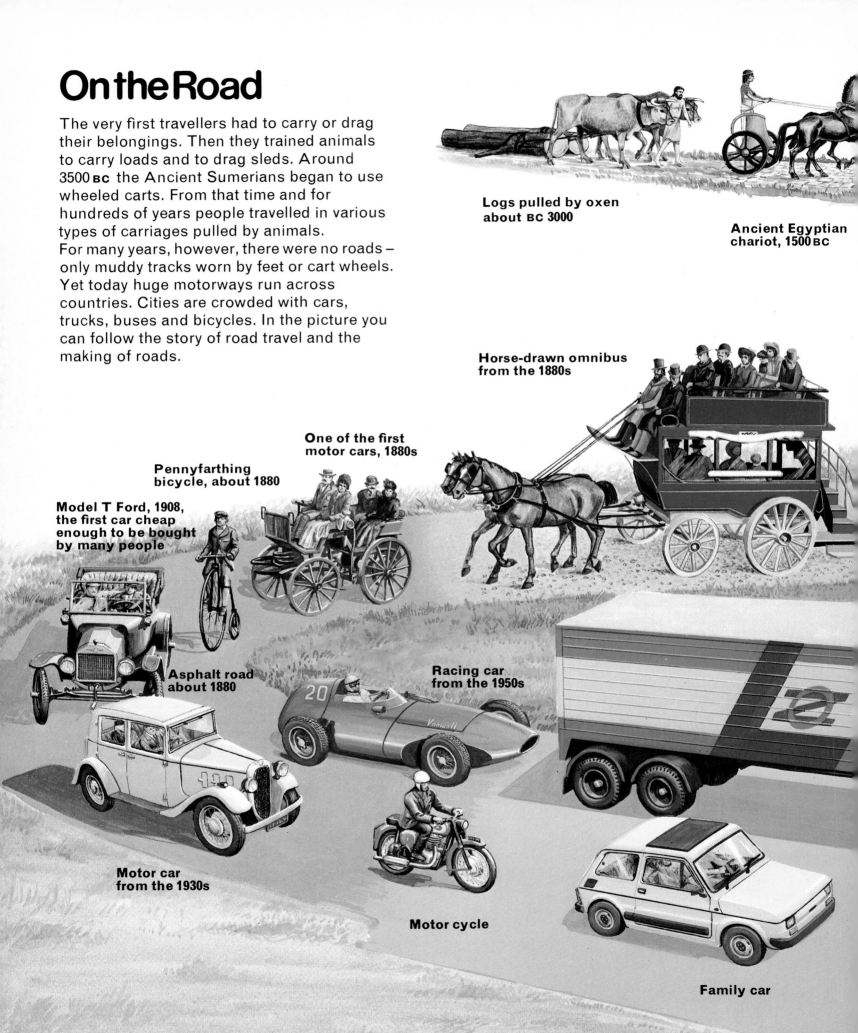

Logs pulled by oxen about BC 3000

Ancient Egyptian chariot, 1500 BC

Horse-drawn omnibus from the 1880s

One of the first motor cars, 1880s

Pennyfarthing bicycle, about 1880

Model T Ford, 1908, the first car cheap enough to be bought by many people

Asphalt road about 1880

Racing car from the 1950s

Motor car from the 1930s

Motor cycle

Family car

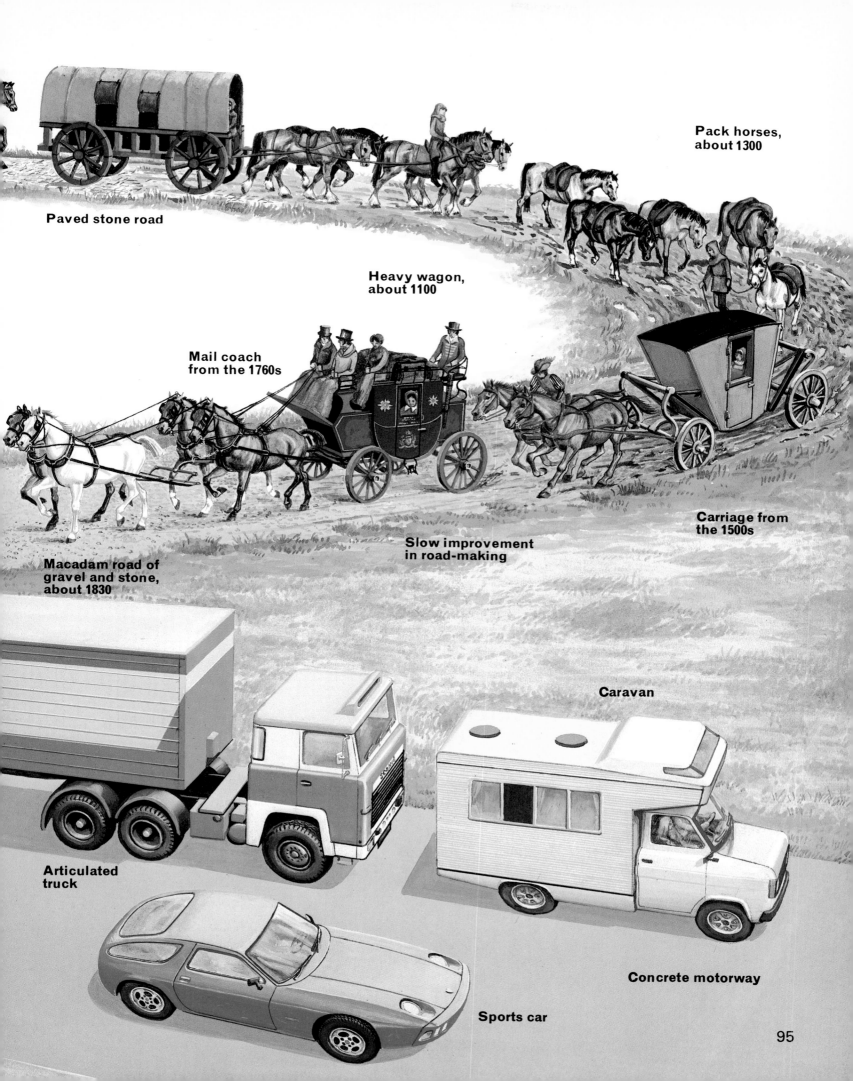

Pack horses,
about 1300

Paved stone road

Heavy wagon,
about 1100

Mail coach
from the 1760s

Slow improvement
in road-making

Carriage from
the 1500s

Macadam road of
gravel and stone,
about 1830

Caravan

Articulated
truck

Concrete motorway

Sports car

95

Railways

The Rocket built by George Stephenson.

LIVERPOOL EXPERIENCE MANCHESTER
RAILWAY · COMPANY

ROCKET

Did you know there were railways long before the steam engine? Horses pulled wagons along metal rails. That way they could move heavier loads. In the 1700s engineers built steam engines to pump water out of mines. Then the steam engine was put on wheels. In 1825 the first all-steam railway was opened and the railway age began. The man who built the *locomotive* (steam engine) was George Stephenson. At first, many people were frightened of the railways. But in a few years rail travel was very popular and railways were built all over the world.

Steam engines were used on the railways for over 100 years. Today, however, there are hardly any left. Diesel and electric locomotives have taken over. Diesel trains are driven by oil-burning engines. Electric trains have motors which pick up current from overhead wires or from a 'live' rail on the track. The first underground railway with steam trains was opened in 1863. Many big cities now have electric trains running in tunnels beneath their streets.

Until the 1900s trains were the fastest means of transport. When the motor car and aeroplane were invented, railways were used less and less. Today there are new trains which travel twice as fast as a car and hovertrains which glide on a cushion of air.

Goods yard

Platform

A city railway station. Both local and international trains stop at the platforms to pick up passengers and mail.

Local train

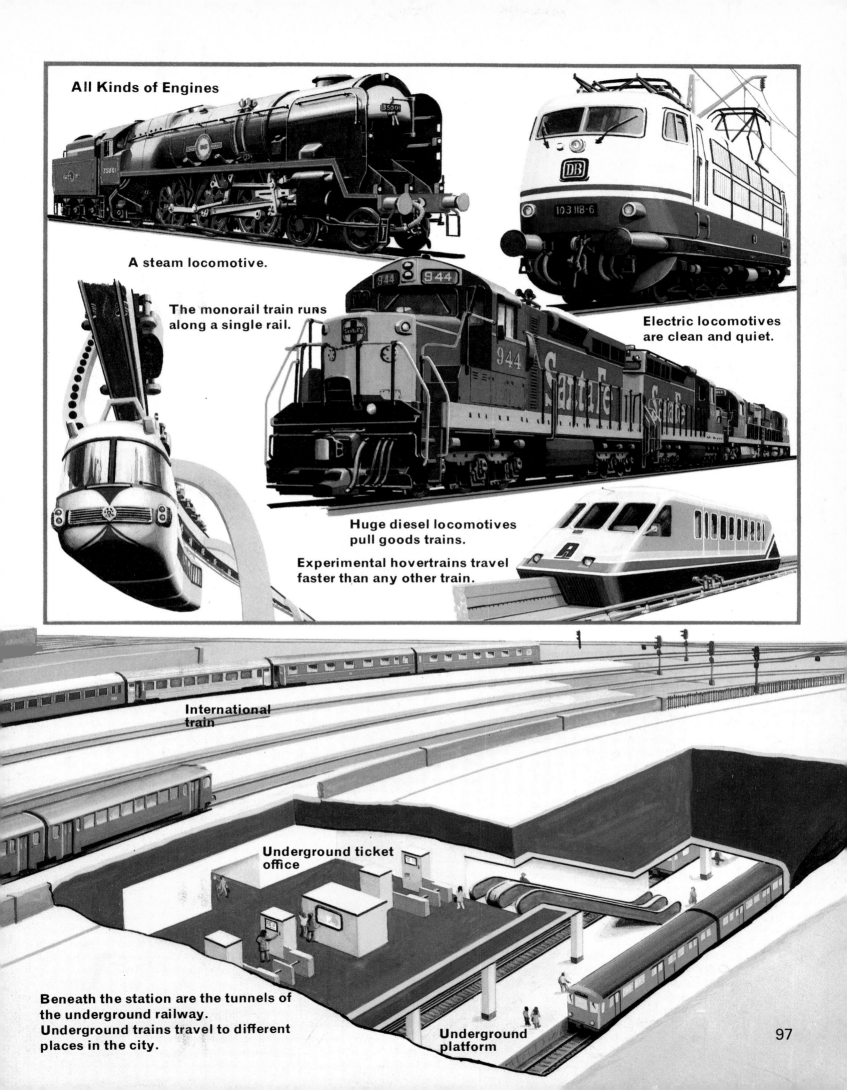

All Kinds of Engines

A steam locomotive.

The monorail train runs along a single rail.

Electric locomotives are clean and quiet.

Huge diesel locomotives pull goods trains.

Experimental hovertrains travel faster than any other train.

International train

Underground ticket office

Beneath the station are the tunnels of the underground railway. Underground trains travel to different places in the city.

Underground platform

97

Boats and Ships

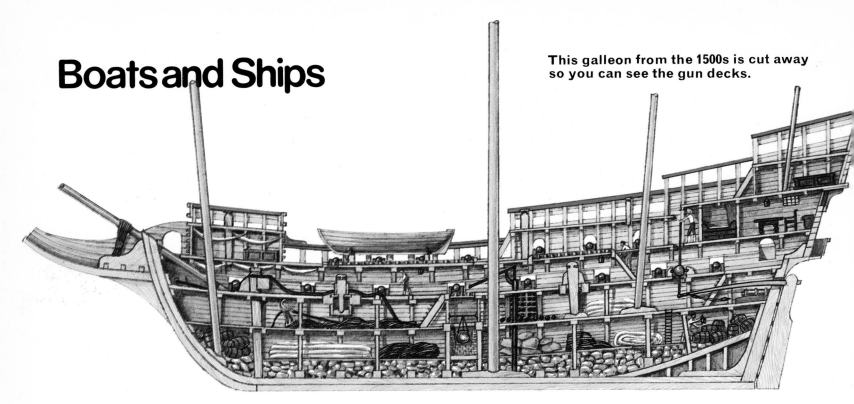

This galleon from the 1500s is cut away so you can see the gun decks.

The first boat was probably a log used by a caveman to help him cross a river. Rafts and canoes followed. Many years later the Ancient Phoenicians, Greeks and Romans built larger boats powered by men and oars. They learnt how to make sails, too, and so use the power of the wind.

In the hundreds of years after this discovery sailing ships of all kinds were built. But in the 1800s steam engines were put into sailing ships and steam ships took over the seas. Today people travel on liners for pleasure and enjoy themselves on yachts and motor boats. Huge cargo ships and super tankers cross the oceans and nuclear-powered submarines travel the world underwater.

Boats and Ships from the Past

Log raft

Clipper

Ancient Greek trireme

Early steamship with paddles

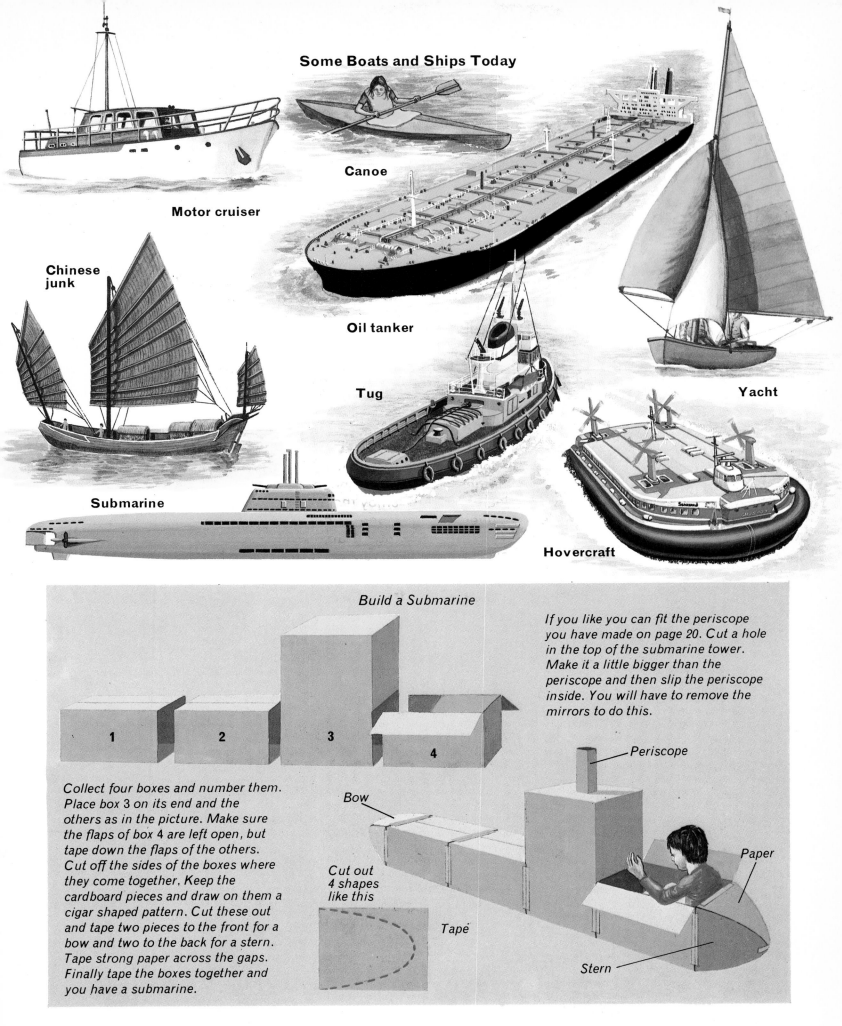

Some Boats and Ships Today

Motor cruiser

Canoe

Chinese junk

Oil tanker

Tug

Yacht

Submarine

Hovercraft

Build a Submarine

If you like you can fit the periscope you have made on page 20. Cut a hole in the top of the submarine tower. Make it a little bigger than the periscope and then slip the periscope inside. You will have to remove the mirrors to do this.

1
2
3
4

Collect four boxes and number them. Place box 3 on its end and the others as in the picture. Make sure the flaps of box 4 are left open, but tape down the flaps of the others. Cut off the sides of the boxes where they come together, Keep the cardboard pieces and draw on them a cigar shaped pattern. Cut these out and tape two pieces to the front for a bow and two to the back for a stern. Tape strong paper across the gaps. Finally tape the boxes together and you have a submarine.

Cut out 4 shapes like this

Tape

Periscope

Bow

Paper

Stern

99

In the Air

Giffard's airship of 1852 had a steam engine.

Otto Lilienthal was a glider pioneer.

Since ancient times people have dreamed of being able to fly. Some people have tried to imitate the birds by strapping on false wings. But they never succeeded in flying in this way. Our bodies are too heavy and our muscles are too weak. The closest we can come to flying like a bird is in a glider.

The first airmen were the Montgolfier brothers, who went up in a balloon in 1783. The next step was to add an engine and make an airship. However, airships were very slow and some exploded!

Other people experimented with gliders. And, in 1903, the Wright brothers made the first flight in a glider, powered by a small petrol engine. The first aeroplane could only just get off the ground. Today people travel all over the world in huge jet planes. And some, like the Concorde, can fly faster than the speed of sound.

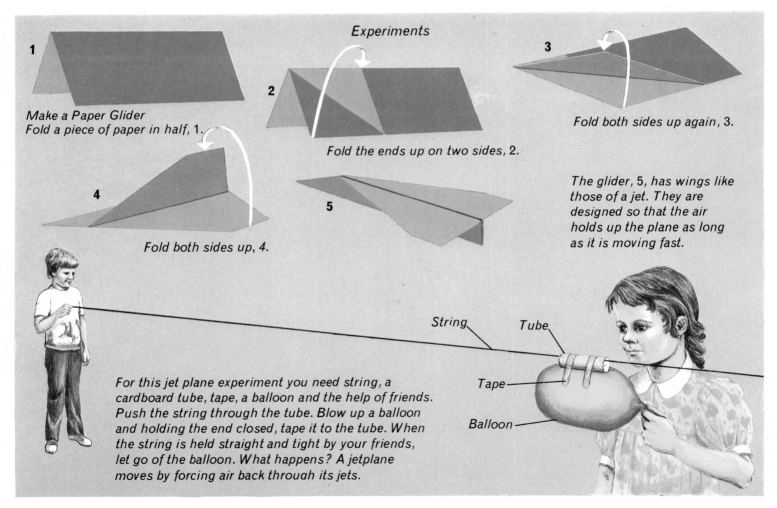

Experiments

1 Make a Paper Glider
Fold a piece of paper in half, 1.

2 Fold the ends up on two sides, 2.

3 Fold both sides up again, 3.

4 Fold both sides up, 4.

5 The glider, 5, has wings like those of a jet. They are designed so that the air holds up the plane as long as it is moving fast.

String

Tube

Tape

Balloon

For this jet plane experiment you need string, a cardboard tube, tape, a balloon and the help of friends. Push the string through the tube. Blow up a balloon and holding the end closed, tape it to the tube. When the string is held straight and tight by your friends, let go of the balloon. What happens? A jetplane moves by forcing air back through its jets.

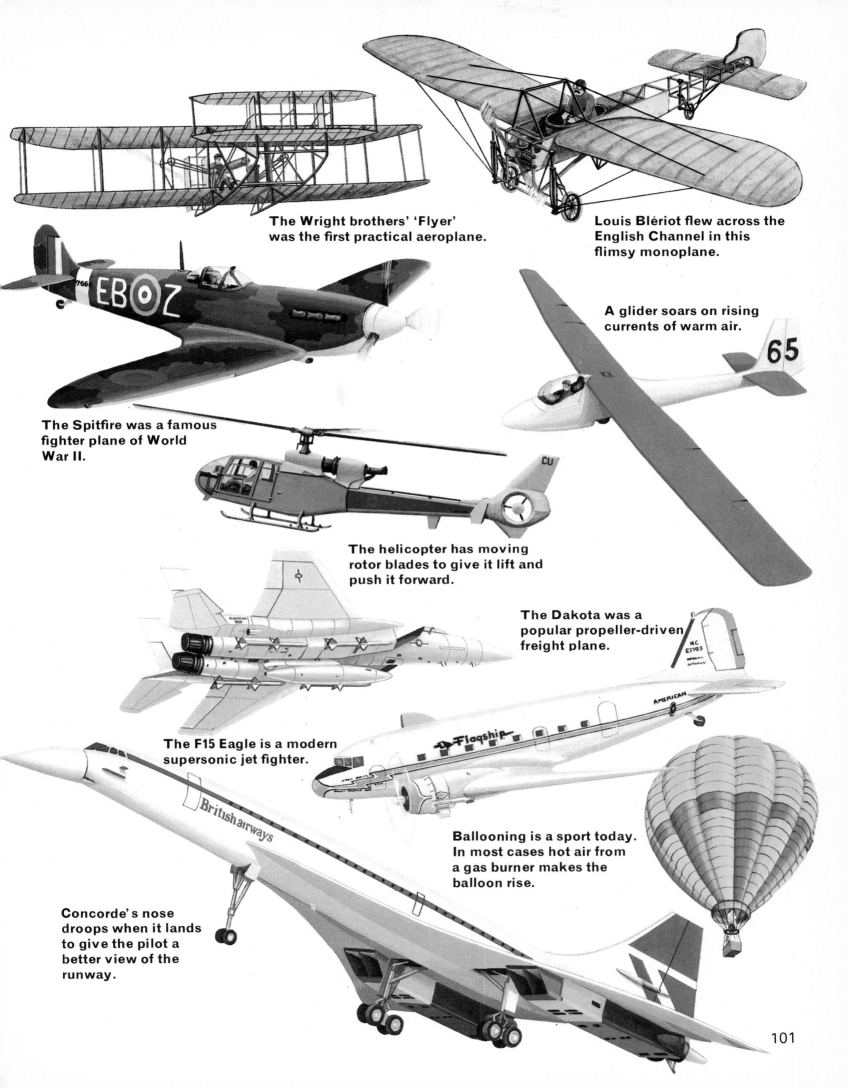

The Wright brothers' 'Flyer' was the first practical aeroplane.

Louis Blériot flew across the English Channel in this flimsy monoplane.

A glider soars on rising currents of warm air.

The Spitfire was a famous fighter plane of World War II.

The helicopter has moving rotor blades to give it lift and push it forward.

The Dakota was a popular propeller-driven freight plane.

The F15 Eagle is a modern supersonic jet fighter.

Ballooning is a sport today. In most cases hot air from a gas burner makes the balloon rise.

Concorde's nose droops when it lands to give the pilot a better view of the runway.

Shapes and Numbers

When we want to keep a score at a football match or measure the area of a floor, we have to answer questions like 'How many' and 'How big'. We have to know numbers and work out space. When we do these things, we are using mathematics.

Mathematics began thousands of years ago when the first farmers had to count their animals or measure their land. When people built houses or canals and bridges, they had to measure and calculate things. As trade grew, merchants had to measure and weigh goods and count money.

To solve problems, short cuts were made. This meant the invention of different kinds of mathematics. They help us today to understand the world. They can also give us games and puzzles to do for fun.

To help us describe an object, we can talk about its shape. Here are some common shapes with the names they have been given by mathematicians.

To draw a circle you need a pair of compasses. A circle drawn on paper is a flat or *plane* figure. Blow it up, like a balloon, and the circle becomes a sphere.

A square is a flat figure too. It has four sides, all the same length. If you blow up a square, you get a cube – like a building block. How many sides has a cube got?

A hexagon has six sides. The sides need not all be the same length. If they are, we say the hexagon is *regular*. Seen under a microscope, a snow flake is a hexagon.

Here is a triangle. Tri means three and all triangles have three sides. A blown up or solid triangular shape is called a *cone* or a *pyramid*. A pine tree is often cone-shaped.

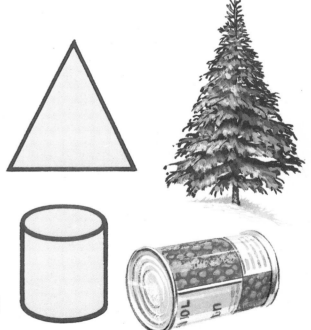

This shape is a rectangle. Only its facing sides are the same length. There are rectangles everywhere. The shoe box is a rectangle. How many more can you find?

A tin is a solid shape. Its ends are alike. They are circles. This shape is called a *cylinder*. Like all solid shapes, a cylinder has an outside surface area and an inside space or *volume*.

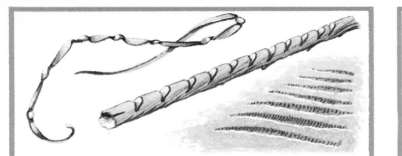

Early people wrote down numbers by making notches on a stick, lines in the ground or knots in a rope. Eventually written numbers were invented. Today we use numbers from an Arabian system used hundreds of years ago.

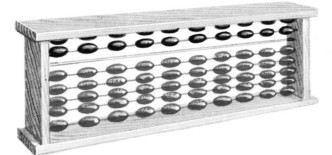

An abacus is an adding machine. It was invented by the Chinese hundreds of years ago and is sometimes used by them today.

Calculating machines like the pocket calculator can do sums at the touch of a button.

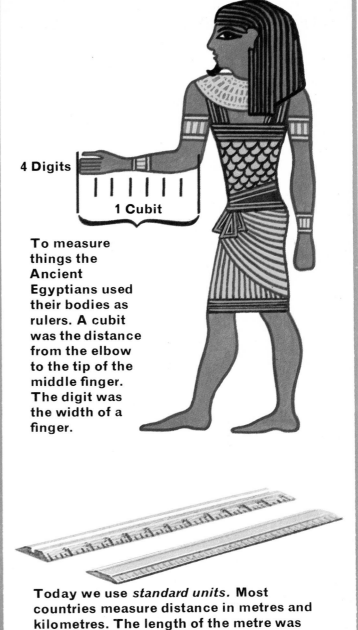

4 Digits

1 Cubit

To measure things the Ancient Egyptians used their bodies as rulers. A cubit was the distance from the elbow to the tip of the middle finger. The digit was the width of a finger.

Today we use *standard units*. Most countries measure distance in metres and kilometres. The length of the metre was fixed by scientists.

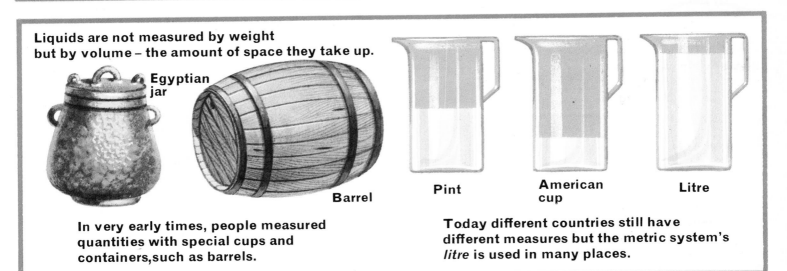

Liquids are not measured by weight but by volume – the amount of space they take up.

Egyptian jar

Barrel

Pint

American cup

Litre

In very early times, people measured quantities with special cups and containers, such as barrels.

Today different countries still have different measures but the metric system's *litre* is used in many places.

Light and Colour

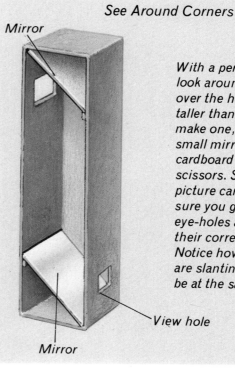

Colour wheel

How We See Colour

Most substances throw back or *reflect* some light waves and take in or *absorb* the rest. In this way our eyes see different colours.

The skin of an orange absorbs all the light waves except orange, which is reflected back.

Coal absorbs all the light waves. No light returns to our eyes. So we see only black.

A sheet of white paper reflects and mixes all the light waves. So we see white.

All light waves can pass through glass (so light passes through clear glass without being changed).

The Sun's light is a white light which is made up of waves of different lengths. These waves travel at enormously high speeds. When sunlight falls on rain, we sometimes see a rainbow of colours. This is because the rain is breaking up the Sun's light into its different wave lengths. A *prism*, like the one in the diagram above, can also split sunlight into its many colours. A simple experiment will show you that white really is a mixture of colours. Make a circle of card and paint it like the card above. Spin it fast and the card will look almost white.

See Around Corners

Mirror

With a periscope you can look around corners or over the heads of people taller than you are. To make one, you need two small mirrors, a tall cardboard box, glue and scissors. Study the picture carefully to make sure you get the eye-holes and mirrors in their correct places. Notice how the mirrors are slanting. They should be at the same angle.

View hole

Mirror

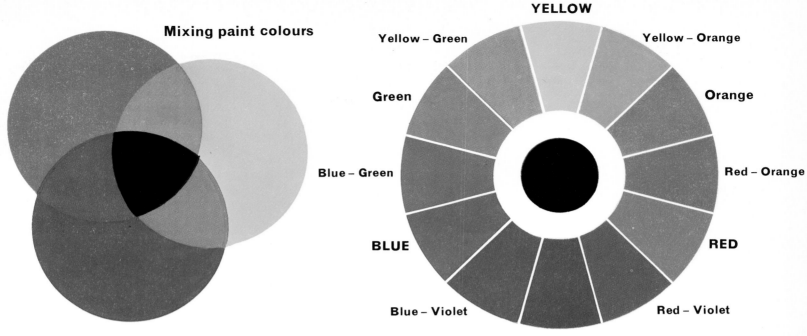

Mixing paint colours

YELLOW
Yellow – Green   Yellow – Orange
Green   Orange
Blue – Green   Red – Orange
BLUE   RED
Blue – Violet   Red – Violet
Violet

We have seen that when the different light colours are mixed they become white. Mixing coloured paints, however, is not the same as mixing light colours. There are three *primary* paint colours: red, blue and yellow. You can mix these to get various colours which you can see in the two colour wheels above. You will see that you cannot get white paint by mixing all the colours but only a dirty black. By adding a little black to a paint colour you get a darker tone. By adding white you get a lighter shade. In this way you can make a large number of colours.

Summer   **Winter**

Some animals use colour as *camouflage*. The Ptarmigan changes colour in summer and winter so that it matches the colour of its surroundings.

Tricks To Play on Your Eyes

Drop a coin into a glass of water. Mark with your finger where the bottom seems to be. If the coin seems to be higher up, this is because water bends light waves. This is called refraction.

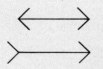

Which line is longer? Use your ruler to check. Your eyes may have been tricked by an optical illusion.

Look hard at the diagram below. Then look away at the ceiling or at a white sheet of paper. What do you see?

Draw a bird on one side of a piece of card and a cage on the other side. Make holes in the card and thread string through. Twirl the string to spin the card. Your eyes hold on to each image for a fraction of a second. So you see both sides of the card at once. The bird goes into the cage.

105

Our Wonderful Bodies

The human body is more wonderful than any machine. It goes on working even while you are asleep. Each of its parts or systems is under the control of the brain.

As you read this, your eyes are sending high-speed messages through your nerves to your brain. When your brain has made sense of the signals, you can 'read' the words written on the page.

Your body is made of millions of tiny cells. It grew from a single cell. Every day of your life, some cells die and new ones take their place. Each cell is fed by the blood pumped around the body by the heart. When you breathe in, your lungs fill with air. The oxygen in the air is used as fuel to burn the food you eat. This gives your body the energy it needs.

You grow up to look something like your parents because your cells have inherited special chemical codes from your parents' cells. Yet, although we look different, we all belong to one human family.

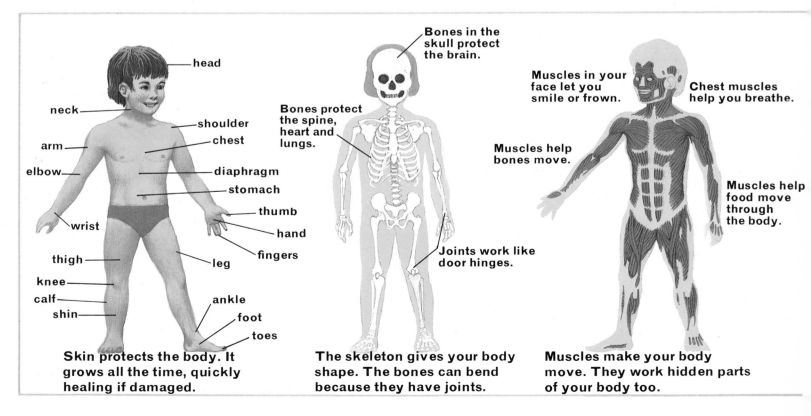

head
neck
arm
elbow
wrist
thigh
knee
calf
shin
shoulder
chest
diaphragm
stomach
thumb
hand
fingers
leg
ankle
foot
toes

Skin protects the body. It grows all the time, quickly healing if damaged.

Bones in the skull protect the brain.

Bones protect the spine, heart and lungs.

Joints work like door hinges.

The skeleton gives your body shape. The bones can bend because they have joints.

Muscles in your face let you smile or frown.

Chest muscles help you breathe.

Muscles help bones move.

Muscles help food move through the body.

Muscles make your body move. They work hidden parts of your body too.

All The Senses

The brain is the most important part of the body. It is the body's command centre. It receives messages along a nerve system. These messages keep inside parts of you, such as your lungs, working. The brain also receives signals from the senses. Our chief senses are sight, hearing, smell, touch and taste.

Inside the nose are sense cells to pick up smells. The nostrils also clean and warm the air you take in to breathe.

The tongue can make sounds. It also has little taste cells or *buds.* These tell us which foods taste sweet and which taste sour.

Eyelashes and eyebrows keep dust and dirt out of the eye. The coloured part of the eye is the *iris.* The dark part is the *pupil.* Light enters the eye through the pupil and touches nerves at the back of the eye. The nerves send messages to the brain, which makes a picture you can see.

The ear picks up sounds. Tiny bones inside the ear vibrate. Nerve cells then send signals to the brain which makes sense of the sounds. Special nerves in the ear help you to keep your balance.

There are nerves all over your body which give you information about anything you touch.

You breathe in fresh air through your nose and mouth.

Air goes through bronchial tubes to the lungs.

The lungs work like bellows, sucking in fresh air and pumping out stale air.

Veins carry used blood from the body to the heart.

Arteries carry fresh blood from the heart to all parts of the body.

The heart pumps used blood to the lungs and fresh blood from the lungs around the body.

Your tongue and teeth help to grind up and mix food.

Special organs in the body make liquids to help digest food.

As food passes through the stomach, the good things are taken out.

The Animal World

All animals have developed, or *evolved*, from very, very simple creatures which lived millions of years ago.

People who study animals have divided all animals into two huge groups. These are the *vertebrates* – animals with backbones and the *invertebrates* – animals without backbones.

Vertebrates

Fish, Frog, Snake, Bird, Panda

Invertebrates

Beetle, Crab, Snail, Jellyfish

These two huge groups of animals are divided into smaller *classes*. An animal class is made up of animals which are alike in important ways. On these two pages are six important animal classes: birds, mammals, reptiles, amphibians, insects and fishes.

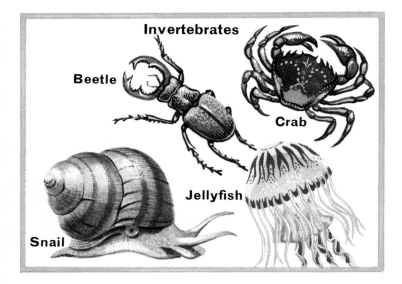

Heron, Ostrich, Budgerigar

All birds have wings, though not all birds fly. Birds have feathers and are warm-blooded. They lay eggs.

Monkey, Seal, Cow, Rabbit

Mammals are the most advanced and intelligent animals. They are warm-blooded and have hair on their bodies. Baby mammals drink milk from their mothers.

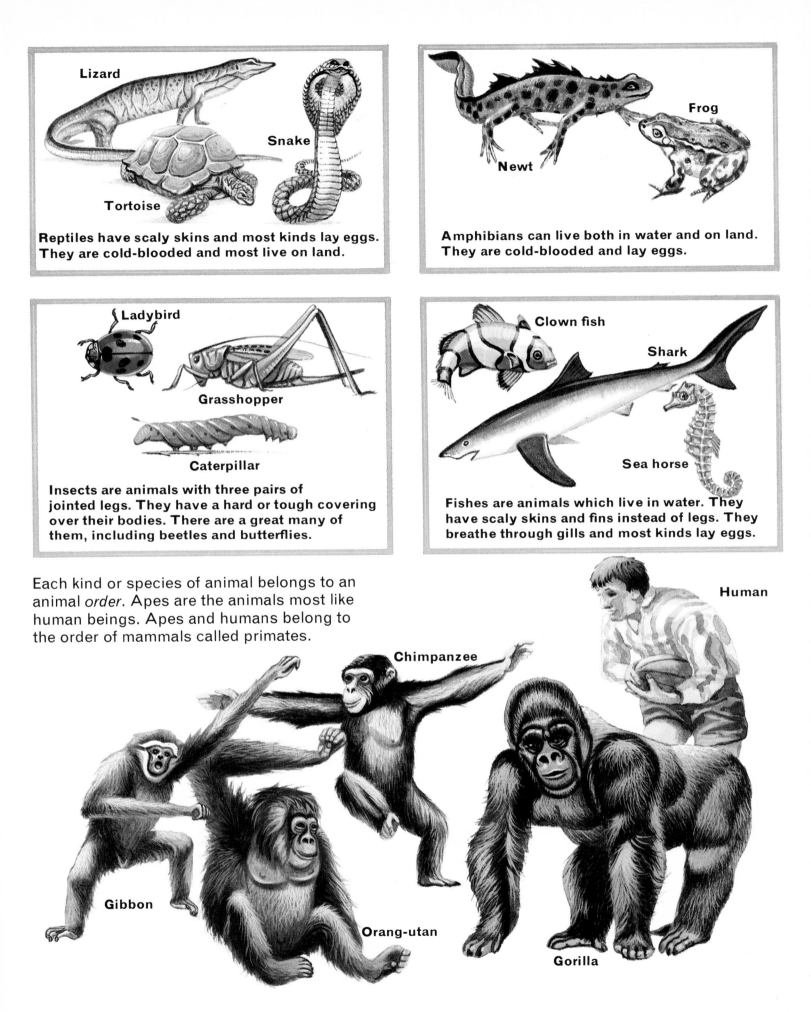

Lizard

Snake

Tortoise

Reptiles have scaly skins and most kinds lay eggs. They are cold-blooded and most live on land.

Newt

Frog

Amphibians can live both in water and on land. They are cold-blooded and lay eggs.

Ladybird

Grasshopper

Caterpillar

Insects are animals with three pairs of jointed legs. They have a hard or tough covering over their bodies. There are a great many of them, including beetles and butterflies.

Clown fish

Shark

Sea horse

Fishes are animals which live in water. They have scaly skins and fins instead of legs. They breathe through gills and most kinds lay eggs.

Each kind or species of animal belongs to an animal *order*. Apes are the animals most like human beings. Apes and humans belong to the order of mammals called primates.

Human

Chimpanzee

Gibbon

Orang-utan

Gorilla

109

Wild Animals

Wild animals live together in communities. The plant-eating animals graze on different kinds of leaves, grasses and fruit. In turn, they are hunted and eaten by meat-eating animals. All kinds of animal are linked with one another by what they eat or what eats them. For example, a rabbit eats grass and a fox will eat the rabbit. We call this the *balance of nature* or a *food chain*.

Animals have adapted to life in many different regions or *environments*. You can see here three different environments.

Animals of the Antarctic have thick coats and layers of fat to keep them warm.

Crab-eater seal

Adélie penguins

Emperor penguin

Many wild animals live in the tropical grasslands or savannas of Africa.

Vulture

Gnu

Elephant

Springbok

Cheetah

Zebra

Rhinoceros

In Australia live the strange platypus, an egg-laying mammal, and the koala and kangaroo. The koala and the kangaroo are marsupials—mammals which carry their babies in pouches.

Platypus

Koala

Kangaroo

Giraffe

Lion

Ostrich

Lioness

In South American rain forests animals live and search for food at different levels in the trees.

Black howler monkey

Macaw

Two-toed sloth

Jaguar

Iguana

Boa constrictor

Birds

All birds have feathers. But not all birds can fly. Some, like the ostrich, have long legs and run away from their enemies. Penguins live in the sea and their wings have become flippers for swimming.

There are nearly 9000 kinds of birds in the world. They live in many different places as you can see in the pictures on the opposite page. Each kind of bird has its own body shape and special type of beak and feet. For instance, the pelican has a pouched beak like a net to catch fish and the greenfinch has a strong beak to crack seeds.

Birds are very light, yet their muscles are strong. They fly by flapping their wings or by gliding on rising currents of air. Small birds can just jump into the air. Big birds need a take-off run.

Watching Birds

Attract birds into a garden with a food table. Make sure it is out of reach of cats. Always provide a dish of water, too.

Coconut

String bag

Blue tit

In winter try and give the birds extra food. Hang up half a coconut. Thread peanuts on a string or stuff a string bag with nuts, seeds, old cake and bacon rinds. You can hang these outside any window too. Do not put out dried coconut or salted nuts, as these could harm birds.

Peanuts

Blackbird

Robin

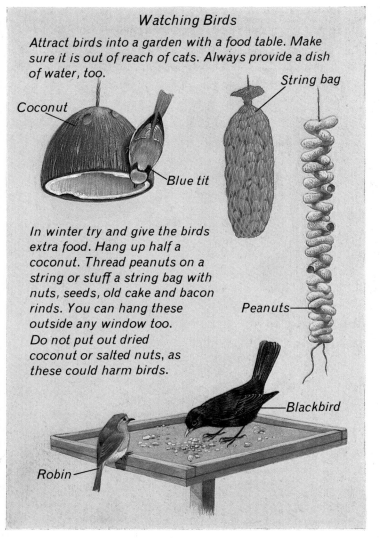

Nests

All birds lay eggs. Nests are built to protect the eggs and chicks. There are some strange nest-builders in the bird world.

The fairy tern balances one egg in the fork of a tree.

The tailor bird uses plant fibres to sew leaves into a hammock-shaped nest.

The weaver bird builds a hanging basket, woven from grasses.

The oven bird shapes an oven-like mud nest.

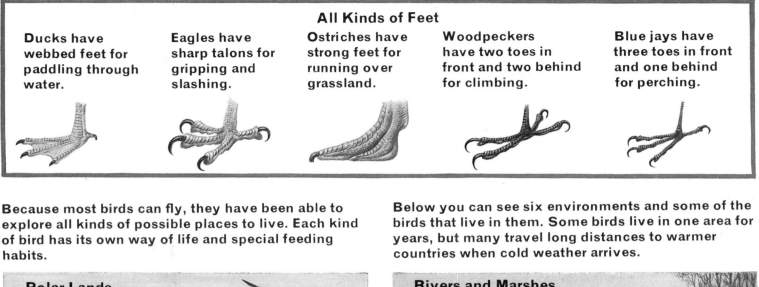

All Kinds of Feet

Ducks have webbed feet for paddling through water.

Eagles have sharp talons for gripping and slashing.

Ostriches have strong feet for running over grassland.

Woodpeckers have two toes in front and two behind for climbing.

Blue jays have three toes in front and one behind for perching.

Because most birds can fly, they have been able to explore all kinds of possible places to live. Each kind of bird has its own way of life and special feeding habits.

Below you can see six environments and some of the birds that live in them. Some birds live in one area for years, but many travel long distances to warmer countries when cold weather arrives.

Polar Lands
Skua
Adélie penguin
Emperor penguin

Rivers and Marshes
Mallard
Swan
Kingfisher

Tropical Forests
Hummingbird
Toucan
Bird-of-paradise

Oceans and Seas
Kittiwake
Pelican
Puffin
Gannet

Woodlands
Woodpecker
Wood pigeon
Owl
Greenfinch

Towns and Cities
House martin
Swallow
Starling
Sparrow

Oceans and Rivers

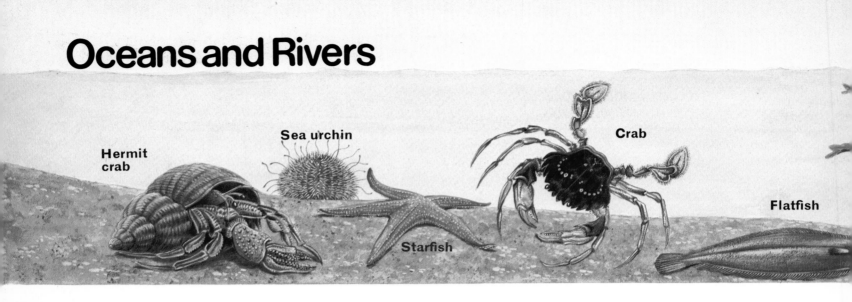

Hermit crab

Sea urchin

Crab

Starfish

Flatfish

Many different creatures live in the water of ponds, rivers, seas and oceans. They can be as tiny as a baby midge or as huge as a whale, the largest animal on Earth. In the oceans, most animals live in the upper sunlit layer. Tiny plants and animals called *plankton* drift here. They are eaten by small sea creatures. In turn these small animals are eaten by larger fishes and whales. Deep down it is cold and dark. Only a few strange creatures live in these depths.

The fresh water of rivers and ponds contains different animals. Some freshwater animals look just like seawater animals but they could not survive in salty sea water. Here, too, you can find very many kinds of animals.

River Life

The picture shows several cold river animals. They are usually found in different parts of a river.

Dragonfly

Beaver

Dragonflies and damselflies are insects that lay their eggs in water.

Trout

Damselfly

Otters and beavers find food and shelter in or near water.

Otter

Frogs and newts are amphibians which lay their eggs in water. The eggs hatch out into tadpoles.

Stickleback

Tadpole

Newt

Frog

Diving beetle

Seaweed

Dolphin

Portuguese man o' war

Manta Ray

Herring

Sea anemone

Barracuda

Tuna

Octopus

Sperm
whale

Conger
eel

Sea horse

Hatchet
fish

Deep-sea
angler

There are many fishes and sea
animals in this picture. But some of
them live in warm seas and some in
cold seas. So you would not find them
all living together like this.

Small Creatures

Bee

Dragonfly

Stag beetle

Mouse

Slug

Snail

Take a secret look at a hidden world – the world of small creatures. Some are so tiny that we need a microscope to see them. Most of the animals in the picture above are insects. There are more kinds of insects than all the other animals put together.

Insects have hard outside cases instead of bony skeletons. Their bodies are jointed, and most kinds have wings. Some insects live in large colonies. The busiest are the ants and bees, which build well-organized homes. Some insects, such as the garden aphid, are pests which do harm. But many are friends, such as the ladybird which eats aphids and so helps gardeners. Many insects change their shape as they grow. First they lay eggs. The eggs hatch into grubs or *larvae*. In time the larvae change into adult insects. Caterpillars, for example, are the larvae of butterflies and moths.

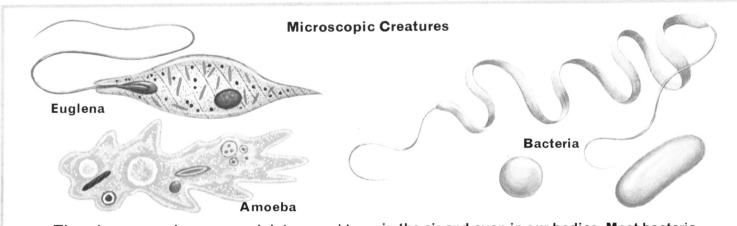

Microscopic Creatures

Euglena

Amoeba

Bacteria

The microscope shows us a miniature world. Only under a microscope can you see tiny creatures called amoeba, one of the simplest animal forms. Even smaller are bacteria. There are millions of bacteria in the soil, in the water, in the air and even in our bodies. Most bacteria are helpful. But some can cause disease. The pictures here show some tiny creatures but, in order to see them, they have been made much, much larger than they actually are.

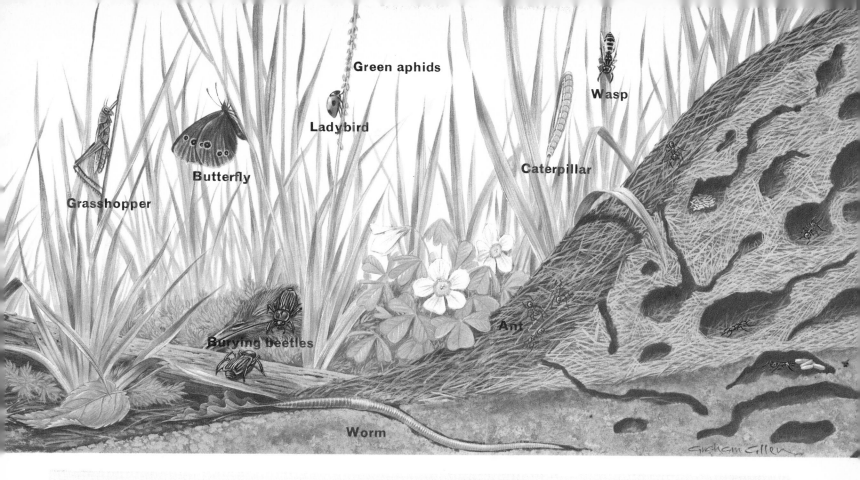

Green aphids

Wasp

Ladybird

Butterfly

Caterpillar

Grasshopper

Burying beetles

Ant

Worm

Finding and Looking After Insects

You can rear caterpillars in a box like the one shown here. Butterflies lay their eggs on plants. Look for them underneath leaves. The caterpillars feed on the leaves after they hatch, so make sure you have a good supply of your caterpillars' food plant. Watch your caterpillars hatch and grow bigger. In time they will turn into chrysalises. Inside the chrysalis, a wonderful change takes place. The caterpillar becomes a butterfly. With luck you may see, after some time, an adult butterfly crawl out of its chrysalis. Free the butterflies and watch them fly away.

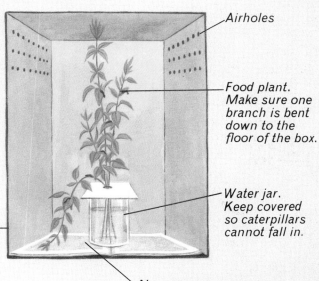

Airholes

Food plant. Make sure one branch is bent down to the floor of the box.

Water jar. Keep covered so caterpillars cannot fall in.

Cardboard box. Wrap cellophane over front.

Newspaper. Change daily.

The Butterfly Life Cycle

Egg

Caterpillar

Chrysalis

Butterfly

To catch insects in a garden, try setting a pitfall trap. All you need is a jam jar. Make a hole deep enough to stand the jar in, so that any insect which falls in cannot climb out. Cover the top with a flat stone raised on pebbles, to stop the trap flooding if it rains. Many insects come out at night to look for food, so check the trap every morning to see what you have caught. It is cruel to keep insects for longer than a day unless you know what to feed them and have made them a special cage. So when you have had a good look at your catches, let them go.

Animals Long Ago

Long before there were people, the Earth was the home of strange prehistoric animals. None of these creatures is alive today. They died out millions of years ago. We know about them because they left their bony *fossil* remains in the rocks.

Life on Earth began 3000 million years ago in the sea. First there were just tiny jelly-like creatures. Then came the first fishes. Amphibians were the first animals to leave the swamps and crawl on land. Slowly after them, the reptiles developed. And for millions of years reptiles ruled the Earth. The greatest reptiles were the dinosaurs or 'terrible lizards'. Some, like Brachiosaurus, were peaceful plant-eaters. Others, like Tyrannosaurus, were fierce meat-eaters. For protection against enemies, Triceratops, Stegosaurus and Ankylosaurus had armoured skins, horns and spiky tails. No-one knows why the dinosaurs died out. Perhaps the climate changed and the plants they ate could no longer grow. The dinosaurs were replaced by mammals. These mammals were much smaller but had bigger brains. They could adjust more quickly to a changing world.

Pteranodon

Apatosaurus
(Brontosaurus)

Brachiosaurus

Dimetrodon

Ankylosaurus

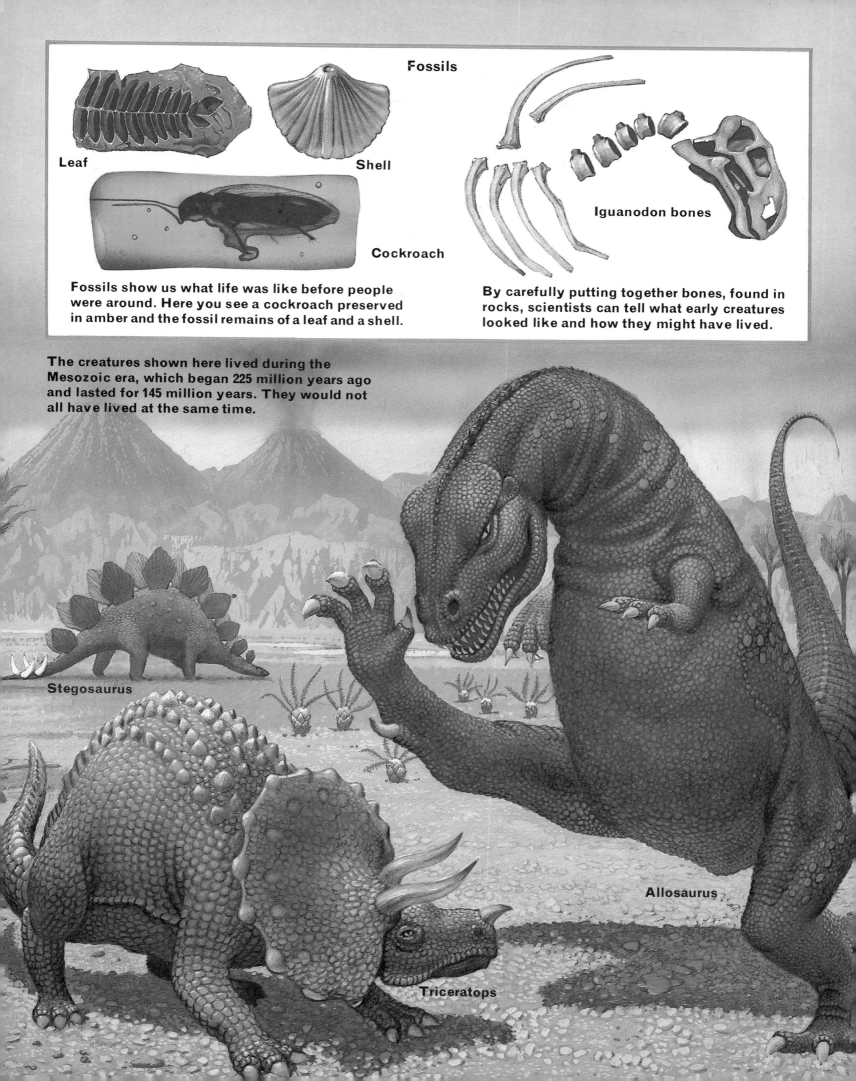

Fossils

Leaf

Shell

Cockroach

Iguanodon bones

Fossils show us what life was like before people were around. Here you see a cockroach preserved in amber and the fossil remains of a leaf and a shell.

By carefully putting together bones, found in rocks, scientists can tell what early creatures looked like and how they might have lived.

The creatures shown here lived during the Mesozoic era, which began 225 million years ago and lasted for 145 million years. They would not all have lived at the same time.

Stegosaurus

Allosaurus

Triceratops

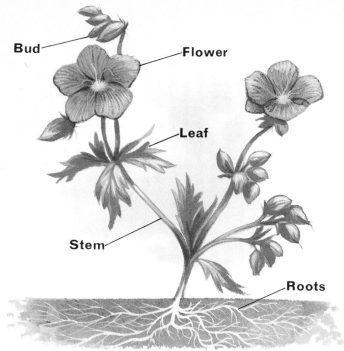

Bud

Flower

Leaf

Stem

Roots

A plant has four main parts – the stem, leaves, roots and flowers. A flower's job is to make seeds so other plants can grow. Follow the pictures below to see how this is done.

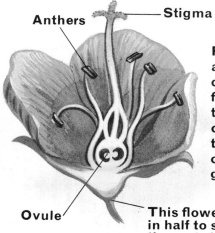

Anthers

Stigma

Ovule

First pollen from the anthers of the same kind of flower must land on the flower's sticky stigma. A tiny tube then grows out of the pollen into a part of the flower called the ovule. The ovule then grows into a seed.

This flower is cut in half to show the parts inside.

Many flowers need the help of insects to bring pollen to them. They get this help by making nectar. Bees and other insects are attracted to this nectar by the smell or colour of a flower. The pollen dust sticks to the the insect and when it flies to another flower, it carries the pollen to the flower's stigma.

The World of Plants

Most plants make new plants. This is done by the plant's flower which makes seeds. After it has been *pollinated* or fertilized, the seeds then grow into new plants.

Many plants live for only one year. However, trees grow larger every year. They have a tough bark to protect them in very cold or hot climates. Many trees that live where winters are freezing cold, shed their leaves in autumn. This helps them save water. Trees which lose all their leaves are *deciduous*. Trees which keep their leaves all year round are *evergreen*.

Seeds

Plants have several ways of spreading their seeds. Some use the wind. Their seeds have wings or fluffy tufts.

Sycamore

Dandelion

Some seeds are carried by animals. Burrs stick to an animal's fur. Other seeds are hidden inside fruits, nuts and berries. The hard seeds pass through the animal's stomach unharmed and fall to the earth.

Blackberry

Hazelnut

Apple

Not all plants make seeds. Fungi (mushrooms and toadstools) and ferns produce spores. Fungi are not green, as they have no chlorophyll. They feed on rotted stuff in the soil.

Mushroom

Fern

Without plants there would be no animals. Plants use sunlight to make food energy. This energy is passed on to animals which eat the plants. Some of these animals are then eaten by other animals, so the energy is again passed on. A plant's roots hold it firm and feed it with salts and water from the soil. With its leaves the plant makes its food. Inside the leaves are green cells containing a substance called *chlorophyll*. This substance and sunlight turn water and carbon dioxide into sugars and starches. The plant 'breathes out' oxygen – the gas that all animals breathe in.

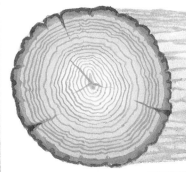

How Old is a Tree?

Each year a tree grows bigger. It adds a ring of new wood beneath the bark. When a tree is cut down, you can tell its age by counting the rings.

An oak is a deciduous tree. In winter the tubes carrying water from the soil to the leaves close up and the leaves die.

Experiments with Plants

Beans are fun to grow. Plant them in a glass jar, close to the edge. Curve a piece of blotting paper inside the glass and keep it damp. This way you will be able to see how the bean starts to grow. Which comes first – the root or the shoot?

Jar

Bean seed

Blotting paper

Try growing vegetables in a shallow dish. Cut the tops off turnips or carrots. Put the tops in a dish of water. Stand the dish in a warm sunny place and soon green leaves will appear. You can try growing potatoes too or the seeds you find in fruit.

All plants need sunlight. You can prove this for yourself if you take two plants and place one on a sunny windowsill and one in a cupboard. Water them both. What has happened after a week?

Carrot   **Turnip**   **Beetroot**

Map Index

Index